FOOD POVERTY & POWER

Mary E.

THE GEOGRAPHY OF HUNGER

"At least half the world's people are still hovering uncertainly in poverty just above starvation level in a world of potential plenty."

Source: *Punch*

FOOD POVERTY & POWER

by Anne Buchanan

Spokesman

First published in 1982 by
Spokesman
Bertrand Russell House
Gamble Street
Nottingham

Copyright© Anne Buchanan 1982

ISBN 0 85124 351 7 Cloth
ISBN 0 85124 352 5 Paper

Printed by the Russell Press Ltd., Nottingham

Contents

Preface

This book is no more than an introduction to some of the political and economic factors which generate hunger throughout the world. Some issues are only touched on but by the use of quotations and references I hope it will serve as a guide to further reading for anyone wanting to find out more about why hunger still exists in a world of plenty.

It is a contribution to the growing debate on food because I think we should (1) stop accepting the present situation as inevitable; (2) inform ourselves of its causes; in order to (3) start opposing the policies, institutions and power structures which maintain the situation at home and abroad.

I would like to thank Keith Buchanan for the constant flow of ideas and encouragement without which this book would not have been possible.

A.B.
Jan 1982

8

Note on terms

Centre, North, Industrialised or **Developed** nations refer to North America, Europe and the USSR, Japan, Australia & New Zealand. South Africa and Argentina are often included with these nations. These countries make up just over 25% of the world's population but get 83% of the world's income.

Periphery, South, Third World, Dependent or 'Underdeveloped' nations refer to Asia, Africa and Latin America — in short, all the rest. These countries make up nearly 75% of the world's population: they have to share just 17% of the world's income.

Although I prefer the neutral term 'South', I have usually used 'Third World' because it is the more familiar term.

Acknowledgements

During 1980/81 I worked for a year on an MSC-funded project on development. This gave me the opportunity to present some of the ideas on which I had been working in a discussion paper. Team work modified and shortened the paper considerably however for the project's needs. The present work grew out of and develops my original ideas.

We are grateful to *Le Monde diplomatique* and du éditions Centurion (publishers of *Pauvres chéris*) for permission to reproduce the cartoons by Plantu. Every effort was made to trace copyright ownership of the cartoons by Vadillo; this proved impossible. We apologise for any possible infringement of copyright.

The cover cartoon is by Vadillo and appeared in *Siempre* (Mexico).

PART ONE:
THE BACKGROUND

"Other farmers and their families, in like plight to ourselves, were also out searching for food; and for every edible plant or root there was a struggle — a desperate competition that made enemies of friends and put an end to humanity."

"For hunger is a curious thing: at first it is with you all the time, waking and sleeping and in your dreams, and your belly cries out insistently, and there is a gnawing and a pain as if your vitals were being devoured, and you must stop it at any cost.... Then the pain is no longer sharp but dull, and this too is with you always, so that you think of food many times a day and each time a terrible sickness assails you.... Then that too is gone, all pain, all desire, only a great emptiness is left, like the sky, like a well in drought...."

Indian famine described by
K. Markandaya: *Nectar in a Sieve*
(Putnam, London 1954)

"1928-9 was a period of famine. The 1928 harvest was bad and, in the spring of 1929, the slave dealers began coming to the villages of northern Shensi. They were out to buy children, and many were sold then.... Most were never heard from again. There was just silence."

Jan Myrdal: *Report from a Chinese Village*
(Heinemann, London 1965)

1. Hunger Amidst Plenty

Famine and malnutrition. We all know the story: they are things that happen to coloured people, people in backward, faraway places. In 1936 Sir John Boyd Orr estimated that, in one particular country, half the population was too poor to afford an adequate diet and one third suffered from serious diet deficiencies. India? China? No. He was referring to one of the richest and most powerful nations in the world: Great Britain. It was happening at a time when others in the country were eating *more* than they needed; and at a time when 'surplus' wheat was being 'disposed of', surplus milk tipped down the drain (Knight & Rotha 1945).

Uneven distribution of food is not a new phenomenon; in 18th century England the labouring population lived almost entirely on cereals and potatoes because they could not afford meat. In his *Diary of a Country Parson 1758-1802*, James Woodforde, who came into direct contact with the poverty of his parish, is greatly concerned about food: "Feb 29 [1788] Mr Taswell sent early to me this morning that he would take a family dinner with us today . . . . It occasioned rather a Bustle in our House but we did as well as we could . . . . We gave the Company for Dinner some Fish and Oyster Sauce, a nice piece of Boiled Beef, a fine neck of Pork roasted, fryed Rabbits, a plumb Pudding and some Tartlets. Desert, some Olives, Nutts, Almonds, and Raisins and Apples . . . . All of us were rather hurried on the Occasion" (OUP 1978: 316-7). In the 19th century, Cole and Postgate tell us, "rural misery had been responsible since 1815 for sporadic outbreaks in years of exceptional distress. Ricks had been burnt, and there had been hunger-riots again and again in the famished areas where *too much food was being produced*" (1938: 233, emphasis added). And as recently as 1935, 62% of army volunteers in the UK, who were mainly working class, did not meet the comparatively low physical standards required.

What do the quotations overleaf tell us about hunger? The first thing, obviously, is that it is the poor who are affected: the rich do not go hungry. As we will show later, hunger is not the result of shortages but rather of political and economic structures which prevent food getting to those who need it: often the very people who grow the crops. The present world economic system requires food to be grown first of all not to feed people but to make a profit; prices must

"Tell me what you earn & I will tell you how you eat."

Hunger is not an unavoidable phenomenon like death and taxes. We are no longer living in the seventeenth century when Europe suffered shortages on an average of every three years and famine every ten. Today's world has all the physical resources and technical skills necessary to feed the present population of the planet or a much larger one. Unfortunately for the millions of people who go hungry, the problem is not a technical one — nor was it wholly so in the seventeenth century, for that matter. Whenever and wherever they live, rich people eat first . . . Hunger is not a scourge but a scandal.

George 1976: 23

Food Consumption by Selected Expenditure Groups in India 1971/2

Expenditure	Calories per consumer unit per day	
(Rupees per head per month)	Urban	Rural
15-21	1582	1957
34-43	2343	3127
75-100	3190	4574

Source: FAO *The Fourth World Food Survey* 1977, Table II.1.3 (2nd, 6th & 9th of 10 divisions in table)

In 1902 in England one survey of domestic budgets showed that upper-class families consumed about three times as much meat per annum as working-class households, four times as much milk and three times as much butter; all of which may go some way to account for the fact that children of twelve years of age who went to private schools were, on average, five inches taller than those who attended State schools.

R. Roberts *The Classic Slum*
(Penguin, Harmondsworth 1973: 119)

be kept high even if it means dumping food needed to keep people
alive. Yet if hunger is the result of man-created structures, and not of
inexorable physical conditions, then mankind can change those

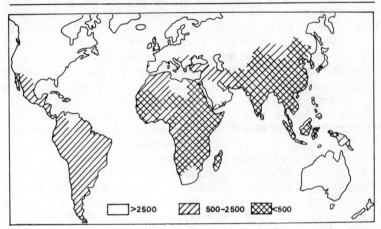

GNP per head (US dollars)

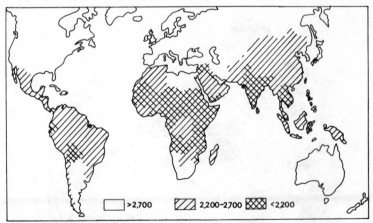

Daily calorie supply per head

"Tell me what you earn and I will tell you how you eat"

This is true at the global as well as at the national or individual level. Note that
both maps show national averages which may conceal very wide differences
within nations.

Data: World Bank Development Report 1980, tables 1 & 22.

structures and eliminate hunger and the poverty with which it goes hand in hand.

This was dramatically illustrated here in Britain just a few years after the situation described above by Boyd Orr. During the 2nd World War, and despite very real shortages, everyone not only had an adequate diet but they actually had a nutritionally better balanced diet than we have today. Sadly, it took the crisis of war to change the conditions of 1936, to force the decision-makers to give people's health a higher priority than profit. Luxuries were cut right back and distribution of essentials to all people was ensured by rationing (including special allowances for children and pregnant women). The crisis enabled Sir John Boyd Orr to promote an agricultural policy which, first, asked what food was needed for the population (not only in terms of quantity but also in terms of protein, vitamins etc), second, saw to it that the food was produced and third, ensured that the people got the food. It was an agricultural policy having as its basis the improvement and then maintaining of the nutritional standards of the population. His vision inspired the 1943 World Food Conference at Hot Springs in the USA which was told that "the goal of freedom from want of food, suitable and adequate for the health and strength of all

"They feed people with words . . ." (see p.18)
Plantu: *Pauvres chéris*, 1978

peoples, can be achieved." The official delegates, from 44 countries, accepted this goal, confident that they could successfully implement it after the war (see Knight & Rotha 1945).

Yet 25 years later Ivan Illich could write: "the majority of men have less food now than in 1945, less actual care in sickness, less meaningful work, less protection.... More people suffer from hunger, pain and exposure in 1969 than they did at the end of World War II, not only numerically, but also as a percentage of the world population" (1971: 165). Of course, throughout history and all over the world there have been famines, bad seasons, lean periods. But these were sporadic, localised. Hunger began to become more widespread among the poor in Europe around the industrial revolution. And what happened in Europe in the 18th and 19th centuries is being repeated on a global scale in the 20th century. Today, and for at least twenty years now, about one tenth of humanity is said to go to bed hungry every night; in the non-Communist Third World one in every four people does not get the minimum needed to stay alive in the long term. In Marshall Sahlins' words: "*This* is the era of hunger unprecedented. Now, in the time of greatest technical power, starvation is an *institution*" (*Stone Age Economics* 1974:36). Why does it happen?

THE FACE OF HUNGER

I counted ribs on his concertina chest
bones protruding as if chiselled
by a sculptor's hand of famine.

He looked with glazed pupils
seeing only a bun on some sky high shelf.

The skin was pale and taut
like a glove on a doctor's hand.

His tongue darted in and out
like a chameleon's
snatching a confetti of flies.

O! child,
your stomach is a den of lions
roaring day and night.

Oswald Mbuyiseni Mtshali
Sounds of a cowhide drum
(OUP, London 1971)

2. Myths About Hunger

Too many people? Too little land?

Among people in the developed countries the most widespread and simple explanation of hunger is that in the hungry countries there are just too many people for the amount of agricultural land available.[1] The solution is then seen as birth control.

There are about 4 billion people living in the world today. If a successful birth control programme (whereby each couple had only two children) could be put into effect immediately the world's population would still not stop growing until next century. This is because of the number of children already born who will reach child-bearing age in the next thirty years. Birth control programmes can thus be effective only in the long term. If the elimination of hunger is seen as a rather more urgent problem then a solution must be found *despite* population increases. Two other points are also important. The first is that people stop having babies when *they decide* they do not want any more, not because of access to techniques of birth control (although such techniques obviously help them implement their decision). And such decisions are made only when hunger is eliminated, when you no longer need six children to ensure a son will be living to look after you in your old age (daughters usually having left home at marriage). In other words, birth rates dropping are the *result* of improvements in living conditions rather than the *cause of* such improvements, which means hunger, not population increase, is the problem to be tackled first. The second point to consider is that the effect of population growth is very different in different parts of the world. If we measure the results by the drain on the world's resources (including food) when each new child is born, then North America's population growth is far more serious than is India's. For the average person in a developed country like the United States of America consumes about forty times the resources used by the average Asian.

---

1. This idea derives from the 19th century theories of the Rev Thomas Malthus, theories rejected by all except those who fear the social change necessary for a more just distribution of the fruits of the earth.

Thus the problem is not people as such but the drain on resources caused by the excessive demands of a rich minority.

The other half of the equation is that there is too little land for the world's population. That this is not in reality an overriding problem is shown by a US Government study which confirms that only 44% of the world's potentially arable land is actually being cultivated (Lappé & Collins 1977: 16). More importantly, the world's farming area could be increased by about 50% without any serious ecological implications such as depletion of forests (George 1976: 299).

And if we look at what is actually being produced right now on the land already cultivated and for the existing world population we might wonder why there is a problem at all. For the world already produces 2 lbs of grain (3000 calories and 65 grams of protein — which is more than the highest estimates of average daily requirements) each day for every man, woman and child on earth (World Bank 1980: 61). 3000 calories a day before we start to count the other staples such as potatoes, cassava or protein-high beans, let alone fruit, vegetables or meat. Furthermore, it has been estimated that we could produce enough on the potentially cultivable area of the globe to support 38-48 billion people: 10-12 times the present world population (Robbins & Ansari 1976: 4) and 3-4 times more than the 12 billion at which it is estimated world population will stabilise within the next century (OECD 1979). In fact, as we know from the varous EEC 'mountains' one of the big problems today is how to get rid of surpluses!

Even though there is enough land for the number of people overall it could be argued that, because people are very unevenly distributed over the earth's surface, some areas are overpopulated. Yet if we look at where people are most concentrated in relation to crop area we see that they are not necessarily the hungry areas. The UK has twice as many people per cultivated acre as has India; Taiwan, which has no serious hunger problem, has twice as many as Bangladesh — the country most people would cite as a clear example of hunger caused by 'overpopulation'. By contrast, much of Africa and Latin America with a low population/land ratio gives us examples of extreme poverty and hunger. But perhaps the best example is that of China; in 1948 William Vogt (in *Road to Survival*, N.Y.) concluded: "There is little hope that the world will escape the horror of extensive famine in China within the next few years"; many other experts agreed. Yet in the 'fifties and 'sixties, with a very much larger population, China not only fed its people but regarded them as its most important resource for, rather than hindrance to, development. The problem is not so much the number of people or the amount of arable land but rather whether the people have the opportunity to grow (and eat) the food they need.

Orient!
The soil on which
    naked slaves
        die of hunger.
The common property of everyone
except those born on it.
The land where hunger itself
    perishes with famine!
But the silos are full to the brim,
full of grain —
        only for Europe.

> Nazim Hikmet in *Selected Poems* (Cape, London 1967)

We had ourselves witnessed the famine in Northern Annam in the autumn of 1931 and seen the unsold consignments of rice piling up on the wharves at Saigon while the authorities refused to succour the famished, thus sowing the seeds of the recent conflict. As early as February 1934 we were unable to pass without comment a proposal put forward by the Association of Wheat Producers in France, which suggested that the 'surplus' rice in Cochin-China should be bought up, like Brazilian coffee, and dropped into the sea. This noble grain, all too scarce in the bowl of the Tonkinese peasant, hindered the marketing of coarse grains at a 'fair' price when it was poured into our pig troughs and fed to our calves and our poultry.

> Dumont 1957: vii

What a bewildering world!
While the fish are drinking coffee in Brazil
babies go without milk here . . .
They feed people with words,
the pigs with choice potatoes.

> Nazim Hikmet *op.cit.*

A hostile environment?

Environmental difficulties are also blamed for hunger: poor soils, erratic climates which cause drought or flood, diseases and pests which ravage the crops. Obviously these are problems. Yet the impact of such factors varies widely between different societies according to the types of technology used and, perhaps more important, the social organization. People starve in Northeast Brazil despite a favourable agricultural environment because of the social organisation which denies access to land for the vast majority. The climate of China did not change yet the catastrophic famine foreseen by Vogt was averted because of social changes which gave land to the peasants and reorganised production and distribution of crops.

Extreme environmental difficulties — drought or crop failure for example — and the deaths associated with them are termed 'natural' disasters. Yet the 'naturalness' of such disaster is questionable. We will look at two such disasters, the Irish famine and the Sahel drought, to see just how far hunger *can* be blamed on environment.

'Natural' disaster? 1. Ireland

From 1845 to 1848 in Ireland, the potato crops, on which the Irish peasants depended for food, failed because they were infested by a fungus called potato blight which caused them to rot, the whole effect being worsened by wet weather which helped the fungus spread. By December 1846 a Cork magistrate touring the country was writing:

"The scenes which presented themselves were such as no tongue or pen can convey the slightest idea of. In the first [hovel], six famished and ghastly skeletons, to all appearance dead, were huddled in a corner on some filthy straw, their sole covering what seemed a ragged horsecloth, their wretched legs hanging about, naked above the knees. I approached with horror, and found by a low moaning they were alive — they were in fever, four children, a woman and what had once been a man. It is impossible to go through the detail. Suffice to say, that in a few minutes I was surrounded by at least 200 such phantoms, such frightful spectres as no words can describe, either from famine or fever. Their demoniac yells are still ringing in my ears, and their horrible images are fixed upon my brain. My heart sickens at the recital, but I must go on . . ." (quoted in Woodham-Smith 1964: 162).

One and a half million people died during the famine and a further million were forced to emigrate, thousands of whom died of disease and starvation in the overcrowded ships; thus Ireland lost two and a half million of its 8 million population in just 4 years.

The underlying causes of this famine are complex but a central factor was the system of landownership in Ireland. Under the tenure laws landlords had complete power to evict tenants and pull down their houses. To pay their rents the peasants grew grain for sale and relied almost exclusively on a diet of potatoes to support their families. Effectively they could not eat their cash crop any more than if it had been the cocoa or tobacco which today puts many peasants in tropical countries in just as precarious a position (see Pyke 1970: ch. 8). And when the peasants, weakened by hunger, due to the failure of their food crop, were unable to grow their cash crops, and thus could not pay their rents, they were evicted in their thousands in Ireland, adding homelessness to hunger. In short, they died, not because of one crop's failure but because, neither owning their land nor having secure tenure of it, they could not make the improvements or grow the range of crops which would have established a healthy farming community able to withstand what should have been a setback but not a disaster.

And that there was nothing, 'natural' about the disaster which followed on the potato crop failures is indicated by the fact that through the worst years of the famine food in the form of cereals and cattle was being exported from Ireland. But the head of the British Treasury, Charles Trevelyan, a stubborn believer in the government's laissez-faire policies, refused to order cereals to be used for relief because he did not wish to "disturb the market". He and his government, like many governments today, were captive to a rigid economic philosophy which puts profit before people; a philosophy in which people are, perhaps, the most easily expendable item. Indeed the government's actions (and inaction) prompted Frank O'Connor to observe: "'Famine' is a useful word when you do not wish to use words like 'genocide' or 'extermination'" (*The Backward Look* London, 1967: 133).

'Natural' disaster? 2. The Sahel

Other examples are numerous but let us take just one recent one: the much publicised Sahel [1] famine of the early 1970s, usually seen as a classic example of a natural disaster caused, in this case, by drought.

As one might expect, the peasants of the region were well aware of the possibility of drought. Meillassoux (1974) tells us that tradionally millet granaries in the Sahel region were constructed to hold four years' consumption and grain was not eaten until it was three years old. Agricultural techniques and cultural traditions were designed to meet possible shortages resulting from unpredictable rainfall. But colonial and modern exploitation (including that by agribusiness) changed this situation. Taxes made cash crops necessary; having less land available then for subsistence crops made the peasants depen-

---

1. The Sahel is a broad belt of land on the southern edge of the Sahara stretching across Mauritania, Senegal, Mali, Upper Volta, Niger, Chad and the Sudan.

Famine is not always the result of an insufficient harvest, but rather of an insufficiency remaining to the farmer after the tax collector, the landlord, and the usurer have taken their share.

André Philip (quoted in De Castro
1952: 156)

The year before the drought they had sold their grain as was usual to the native store . . . [He] sent his men around the native villages, coaxing them to sell everything they had. He offered a little more money than they had been used to get. He was buying at half of what he could get in the city. And all would have been well if there had not been that season of drought. For the mealies wilted in the fields, the cobs struggled towards fullness, but remained as small as a fist. There was panic in the villages and the people came streaming towards the Greek store and to all the other native stores all over the country. The Greek said, Yes, yes, he had the maize, he always had the maize, but of course at the new price laid down by the Government. And of course the people did not have the money to buy this newly expensive maize.

Doris Lessing *Hunger* in
Five Short Novels (Panther, St Albans 1969)

The poor do not necessarily starve because there is no food around, but because they simply do not have the buying power to acquire it. So, hunger and poverty cannot ipso facto be eliminated by producing more. What needs greater attention is how to empower the poor so that they may get their due share; for when the chips are down those who have power (land and other assets) survive, those who are powerless perish.

Malik 1980

dent in part at least on the market for their food; and having to buy food in turn meant the necessity for more cash crops. Thus when drought struck the peasants had no reserves. Yet the food was there. Lappé and Collins, using FAO statistics, tell us that many food exports from the Sahel actually increased during the drought: "Cattle exports from the Sahel during 1971, the first year of full drought, totalled over 200 million pounds, up 41 per cent compared to 1968. The annual export of chilled or frozen beef tripled compared with a typical year before the drought. In addition 56 million pounds of fish and 32 million pounds of vegetables were exported from the famine-stricken Sahel in 1971 alone" (1977: 102), most going to consumers in Europe and North America. (Indeed the World Bank sees the region's future as a major vegetable producer for the North American and European markets.) The impact of the big cash crops can be seen in the figures for Mali: between 1967 and 1973 food crop production fell from 60,000 tonnes to 15,000 tonnes while, over the same period, groundnut exports rose from 8,000 to 11,000 tonnes and cotton exports increased from 3,165 to 22,000 tonnes. Yet even with this distortion of the agricultural economy "every Sahelian country, with the possible exception of mineral rich Mauritania, actually produced enough grain to feed its total population even during the worst drought year" (Lappé & Collins 1977: 104). Thus the famine was not caused by any overall shortage of food; rather was it caused by powerful indigenous elites and outside business groups who were able to manipulate the food situation to their own profit (see Meillassoux).

The ordinary people starved as the following sequence of events worked its way through. The taxes which fall immediately after the harvest (and repayment of debts) force the peasants to sell much of the food which they should store for the lean time before the next harvest. Profiteers who pay low prices at this time of plenty then sell back at high prices at the later time of demand, often forcing the farmer to obtain credit at usurious rates of interest. Even if not actually forced from their land the farmers certainly are unable to improve their land (for example, by irrigation, for which, with its major river systems, the Sahel has a great potential) and gradually exhaust their soils. Then, with drought, the profits increase for the few and the small farmers and labourers, poverty stricken and unable to buy the very food which they have produced, starve.

A similar story could be told about Bangladesh. But the reality is clear enough: "Natural calamities may point up the weaknesses of underlying social structures, but they do not *cause* them" (George 1976: 44). As a group of researchers from the University of Bradford's Disaster Research Unit conclude: "The time is ripe for some form of precautionary planning which considers vulnerability of the population as the real cause of disaster — vulnerability that is induced by socio-economic conditions that can be modified by man, and is not just an act of God" (O'Keefe *et al* 1976: 567). So, having seen that the commonly given reasons for hunger just do not explain anything satisfactorily, let us take a look at these "underlying social structures".

THE EARTH IS A MOON SATELLITE

Apollo 2 cost more than Apollo 1
Apollo 1 cost plenty.

Apollo 3 cost more than Apollo 2
Apollo 2 cost more than Apollo 1
Apollo 1 cost plenty.

Apollo 4 cost more than Apollo 3
Apollo 3 cost more than Apollo 2
Apollo 2 cost more than Apollo 1
Apollo 1 cost plenty.

Apollo 8 cost a fortune but nobody minded
because the astronauts were Protestants
and from the moon they read the Bible
to the delight and edification of all Christians
and on their return Pope Paul gave them his blessing.

Apollo 9 cost more than all of them together
and that includes Apollo 1 which cost plenty.

The great-grandparents of the Acahualinca people
were less hungry than the grandparents.

The great-grandparents died of hunger.

The grandparents of the Acahualinca people
were less hungry than the parents.

The grandparents died of hunger.

The parents of the Acahualinca people
were less hungry than the people are today.

The parents died of hunger.

The people who live today in Acahualinca
are less hungry than their children.

The children of the Acahualinca people
are not born because of hunger
and they hunger to be born
so they can die of hunger.

And that is what the Acahualinca people do
they die of hunger.

Blessed are the poor
for they shall possess the moon.

Leonel Rugama (Nicaragua)
Published in *Spes*, Montevideo, Jan 1970
Translation by Gary MacEoin

3. Historical Roots of Hunger

We have seen that in areas of hunger or famine, whether in England or Ireland on the one hand or Third World countries on the other hand, it is the poor who starve while there is always plenty of food for those with the money to pay for it. This is because the people who control or own the land are interested in food not primarily as something to be eaten but rather as something which is bought, sold and gambled with for profit. And if the profits are greater from non-food crops then there is no *economic* reason why land should be used to grow food at all. Lappé and Collins (1977: 266) note that two and a half acres planted to carnations in Colombia give a profit 80 times greater than the same area planted in wheat or corn. As the big estates and corporations take over more land, the peasants are bought out and driven off the land to swell the increasing numbers of shanty-town dwellers in the giant cities of the Third World where, with no land and massive unemployment, they are trapped in a desperate situation. How does this situation come about?

Government are prepared to unite men and resources for a world war but the Great Powers are not prepared to unite to banish hunger and poverty from the world . . . The story of the economic domination of the earth, and the exploitation of the people and natural resources of weak nations by western European nations in the last three hundred years and since the Spanish American war by the United States . . . is a shock to anyone with preconceived ideas of the glories and virtues of our western civilisation. It is a story of a ruthless fight for wealth with little regard for the rights or welfare of 'inferior races'.

Sir John Boyd Orr, Foreword to
de Castro 1952: 7

Today food is gambled with and manipulated for the profit of the few.

The Inheritance of Colonialism

Many Third World countries until recently have been colonies of the developed nations. The impact of this colonization was complex and the reasons for it varied. But some elements in the process are straightforward. The enormous industrial development of the rich nations in the late 18th and the 19th centuries depended on many workers being freed from agricultural work to go and work in industry in the cities. This meant that they had to be fed from elsewhere and preferably on cheap food so that wages could be kept low and profits could be kept high. So colonies were necessary for cheap food (e.g. tea from India or wheat from Canada). They were also necessary for raw materials. Thirdly, they were used to generate the capital necessary for the expansion of 19th century industry, from the profits which came from crops such as tobacco, cotton, cocoa, tea, coffee and sugar. And fourthly they were necessary as markets for the industrial goods being produced in Europe (a market opened up by the destruction of the industries of the colonies — see the Indian case study below). In short, the industrialised nations grew rich by inducing the colonised countries to stop producing what was sensible and necessary as far as they were concerned and instead produce what we wanted — to develop and maintain a high standard of living and enormous profits

Plantu in *Le Monde diplomatique*

Unless the structures of oppression which cause poverty and hunger — as typified by local military and business groups and their outside collaborators — are ended, the most well-meaning aid is useless.

for the few who held economic and political power. This resulted for the Third World in what is termed 'dependent development' — that is, development dependent on the Centre (although, in truth, it is rather the Centre's development which has been dependent on the exploitation of the Periphery). Although most of the former colonies are now politically independent the pattern continues very much the same because they have inherited warped economic structures and because the elites to whom power was handed over on independence have every reason to continue the system of the former colonisers and thus share in the profits which still drain out of the poor nations to the rich ones.

Thus we see that there are not really two different groups of nations — one 'developed' and the other, because of some internal deficiency on their part, 'underdeveloped'. Rather, the two sets of nations are part of the same system, two sides of a single coin. The development of the Centre has been achieved only by the *mal*-development of the Periphery, by the transfer of wealth from one to the other. This process can also be seen at work *within* each sector: for example, the Irish peasants were a 'Periphery' to the economic and political power of the London 'Centre'; and the elites in the Third World today can be seen as part of the 'Centre' to which they owe allegiance and with whom they have more in common than with the peasantry or 'Periphery' of their own nations.

Everywhere there are banquets and festivities,
Delicious roast chicken is set before them [the elites],
Chicken from the village where prosperity was promised.

Father Utih still waits in prayer,
Where are the leaders going in their limousines?

Usman Awang
Modern Malay Verse (OUP, Kuala Lumpur 1963)

Today, Third World elites and giant transnational corporations (also called 'multinationals') take the place of the colonisers, owning or controlling vast tracts of land on which the highly profitable export crops are grown. For example, as Susan George tells us, "about fifty five per cent of the entire Philippine farming acreage is used for export crops — sugar, coconuts, rubber, pineapple, coffee and cocoa —much of it directly controlled by foreign interests in cooperation with a tiny local elite" (1976: 172). And so the inequalities continue to grow, the result, as Dumont and Cohen stress, of "the removal of control over production from those who work the land into the hands of those who merely speculate on and profit from it" (1980: 27). These inequalities today divide the world into those who eat and those who hunger.

India: Classic Colony

In the 18th century when the British colonised it, India had a healthy agricultural sector backed up by a widely dispersed and prosperous craft industry; its exports (including various textiles and metalwork), valued at over 6 million pounds sterling a year, were going to Europe, North Africa and China.[1] It was economic pressure applied by the British which destroyed this thriving manufacturing sector. On one hand the British East India Company gained a virtual monopoly over the buying of India's exports and "began to force the artisans to sell at prices so low that they 'brought on the complete ruin of Indian industry and commerce' " (De Castro 1952: 158). Meanwhile, the British government wished to protect the growing textile industry in Britain; this could not compete with Indian imports because, until 1813, they were sold at about half the price of the British product. It therefore began to levy heavy duties on Indian imports of around 70% of the product's value. Thus Indian goods were taxed out of the British market while British goods circulated freely in India; it meant the death knell of Indian manufacture: "Had this not been the case," wrote Horace Wilson, "the mills of Paisley and Manchester would have been stopped in their outset, and could scarcely have been again set in motion, even by the power of steam. They were created by the sacrifice of Indian manufacturers" (quoted in Clairmonte 1960: 87). As a result of these measures, between 1814 and 1835, British exports of cotton goods to India increased, in terms of yardage, from 818,208 to 51,777,277. The value of Indian cotton goods exports fell from £1,300,000 in 1814 to £100,000 in 1832. "Indian spinners, weavers and metal workers were driven out of business . . . . The population of Dacca, Surak, Murshidabad and other manufacturing centres, was decimated in a generation. 'The bones of the weavers,' said an English Governor-General, 'were bleaching the plains of India'" (quoted in Wheelwright 1968: 57).

Nor was India's agriculture underdeveloped. In 1893 a British agricultural scientist who had been sent to India reported that "nowhere would one find better instances of keeping land scrupulous-

1. The scale of these exports can be judged from the fact that Britain's total national income in 1770 was only £125 million.

> The Hindoo may well say that nothing is left him but his skin. He knows no freedom but to die: yet he is the subject of England, whose people are furnishing the world with missionary bishops to teach Christianity, the basis of which is "Do unto your neighbour as ye would that he should do unto you" . . . The Hindoo raises cotton, but consumes only so much as will give him a strip to cover his loins. He raises rice, but he eats little for he may not even clean it: and all this is done that England may be the workshop of the world . . .
>
> Henry Carey (1848) quoted in
> Clairmonte 1960: 112-3

ly clean from weeds, of ingenuity in device of water-raising appliances, of knowledge of soils and their capabilities, as well as of the exact time to sow and reap, as one would find in Indian agriculture . . . . It is wonderful, too, how much is known of rotation, the system of 'mixed crops' and of fallowing . . . . I, at least, have never seen a more perfect picture of cultivation" (quoted in Lappé & Collins 1977: 77).

But the destruction of Indian industry forced India into an increasing dependence on agriculture: from 1891 to 1931 alone the population dependent on agriculture rose from 61% to 75%. As the artisans were driven back to the land the size of rural holdings fell, pressures on the soil increased and "hunger took possession of the whole country" (De Castro 1952: 159). Meanwhile, on colonisation, the British had introduced a landlord system known as the Permanent Zemindari Settlement. Existing Zemindars, who collected land tax on a commission basis, were made permanent landlords; this gave them enormous power and led to corruption and rack renting. The 1880 Famine Commission noted with alarm that the increasing number of tenants-at-will "are kept in a situation of absolute dependence on the landlord, which takes away the desire to improve the land, or to raise their own position, or to lay by anything from the profits of agriculture. The soil, therefore, is not unlikely under such tenants to become year by year less productive; and the tenant having neither credit nor stores to fall back upon becomes a prey to the first approach of famine" (quoted in Clairmonte 1960: 101). Clairmonte, summing up the effects of colonisation on India, concludes: "The systematic destruction of Indian manufactures; the creation of the

Zemindari and its parasitical outgrowths; the changes in agrarian structure; the financial losses incurred by tribute; the sharp transition from a pre-monetised economy to one governed by the international price mechanisms — these were some of the social and institutional forces that were to bring the apocalypse of death and famine to millions" (p.107). Thus the hunger of India is neither inevitable nor accidental but has its roots in the 'dependent' development resulting from the country's colonial status.

If security was wanting against popular tumult or revolution, I should say that the 'Permanent Settlement' though a failure . . . in most important essentials, has this great advantage, at least, of having created a vast body of rich landed proprietors deeply interested in the continuance of British Dominion and having complete command over the mass of the people.

Lord William Bentinck,
Governor-General of India, 1829-35
quoted in Clairmonte 1960: 98-9

---

4. 'Dependent' Development

What is underdevelopment?

A dwarf with an enormous head and a swollen chest is 'underdeveloped' in the sense that his weak legs and short arms do not correspond to the rest of his anatomy; he is the monstrous product of a malformation that distorted his development. That is what we, the kindly named 'underdeveloped' countries, are in reality, countries that are colonial, semi-colonial or dependent. Ours are countries with distorted economies, distorted by imperialist policy, which has abnormally developed the industrial or agricultural branches that complement the imperialists' own complex economies. 'Underdevelopment' or distorted development brings a dangerous specialisation in raw materials that keeps all our people in peril of hunger. We, the underdeveloped, are also the countries of monoculture, of the single product, of the single market.

Che Guevara in *Monthly Review*
(New York) July-August 1961

The 'dependent' development of Third World countries affects every aspect of society; in relation to food supplies we will look at five major results.

1. Uneven development of the infrastructure

Along with the deliberate encouragement of export crops there was a very uneven development of the infrastructure of colonised countries — e.g. the railways, roads and port facilities — which was designed to serve the export economy, to siphon out raw materials and to distribute imports. Eduardo Galeano, speaking of Brazil's railroad system, comments: "The tracks were laid not to connect internal

areas one with another, but to connect production centres with ports ..
.. Each Latin American country still identifies itself with its own port
— a negation of its roots and real identity — to such an extent that
almost all intraregional trade goes by sea; inland transport is virtually
non-existent." And he concludes that the railroads "were an imped-
iment to the formation and development of an internal market" (1973:
282, 218). Colonised countries in Asia and Africa repeat the pattern.

2. Lack of food self-sufficiency

The increasing amounts of good land taken over for export crops
meant that staple food crops were pushed onto smaller areas of more
marginal land with the result that many Third World countries have
become less and less self-sufficient in food and have to rely
increasingly on imported food. The process, started last century, still
continues: while Third World nations could still export 12 million
tons of grain a year in the 1930s, by the late 1970s they had to *import*
nearly 80 million tons (ICIDI 1980: 91). In Latin America, per capita
production of subsistence crops decreased by 10% between 1964 and
1974 while production of export crops increased by 27% (*NACLA
Report* Jan-Feb 1978: 5). The food imported to fill the resulting shortfall is, of course, more expensive than that a peasant could grow and
those who cannot afford it do not eat.

'Development' through hunger

It was not the hunger of rebels left to die in jail; it was the
hunger of slaves who allowed themselves to be killed....
It was not the hunger of the unemployed; it was the
hunger of desperately overworked peons.
It was not unproductive hunger; it was hunger which
filled the granaries of the Sierra to bursting point and
brought new grist to the mills of the capitalist aristocracy.

Jorge Icaza *Huasipungo*
(Dobson, London 1962)

---

3. Uneven nutritional levels

The third result of dependent development is an increasing skewing of
nutritional levels, involving not merely the quantity of food eaten (as
measured by the number of calories) but also the nutritional value —

the balance between carbohydrates (sugars and starches), fats, proteins, vitamins and minerals. United Nations data underline the extreme inequality in food intake between the developed and under-developed nations. Not only does the developed world eat more food totally and more protein, but it gets its protein from animal rather than vegetable sources to a much higher degree than does the Third World. And because, under intensive rearing, it takes many pounds of grain to produce 1 lb of animal protein (beef, chicken, eggs etc), the average person in the developed countries eats about 2000 lbs of grain a year although less than one-tenth of that is consumed directly (mostly as bread). The average consumption in the poorer countries is about one-fifth that of the developed countries but most of it is eaten directly as grain. Dumont and Cohen tell us that "nearly a third of the world's grain supplies are fed to livestock . . . . Overall, the richer countries, including the USSR, give more grain to their livestock each year than is available for the combined human and animal populations of the poorer countries" (1980: 137). And the result of diverting so much grain from people to animals is brought home by their comment that "a tenth part of the grain fed to beef cattle in 1974 could have met the entire grain shortfall in Asia" (p.138). Similarly, other foods such as skim milk, oil cake and fishmeal are fed to animals: in Peru, for example, fish has become too expensive for the poor because fishmeal to feed the animals of North America and Europe is a major export. And in the 1960s the Netherlands was feeding more skim milk to its livestock than UNICEF and food aid programmes were distributing (Dumont & Cohen 1980: 138-9).

An aside on protein

Before we look at the fourth effect an aside on protein is needed. If a Western-style diet, high in animal protein, was necessary to ensure the health of the Third World then the outlook would indeed look grim. But there are several considerations here. Firstly, to obtain even animal protein it is not necessary to use the vast amounts of feedstuffs which the rich nations use. As Susan George comments: "If the Chinese, who raise about four times as many pigs as the Americans, collectively went mad tomorrow and began to feed their pigs on grain as Americans do, there would be very little grain left in the world for humans anywhere" (1976: 24). The point is that animal protein (though less of it) can be — and used to be — produced in less extravagant ways, e.g. sheep rearing on land marginal for arable cultivation. The second point is that many grains and vegetables are good sources of protein but this has been generally overlooked in the West where animal protein has more status. And thirdly the whole

THE COST OF ANIMAL PROTEIN

Bread □

Eggs □□□□

Milk □□□□□

Beef □□□□□□□□□□

Chicken □□□□□□□□□□□□

Production of animal protein is extravagant in terms of grain. The squares of the diagram represent the number of calories of grain required to produce one calorie of the foods listed; i.e. to produce one calorie of chicken meat demands 12 calories of grain. The animal-protein-rich diets of the wealthy nations are thus possible only by the diversion of grain from human consumption. The figures on which the diagram is based are taken from Strahm but would be regarded as conservative by other writers on the food problem.

concept of protein shortage in the Third World is a complex and controversial one. Colin Tudge argues that if people are getting enough of their staple food then they are generally getting enough protein, but that if the *amount* of food eaten is too small then protein will be burnt as energy to compensate for lack of carbohydrate and thus cannot perform its real protein function of body building. In other words he says more food is usually the answer, not more protein (1979: 69-85).[1] By contrast most people in the developed societies have a protein intake far in excess of need and could drastically cut their consumption of meat with no adverse health effects.

4. Impact on the balance of payments

Dependent development has a major impact on the balance of payments of a nation i.e. the balance between the money going out of a country, for example to pay for imports or to service debts, and the money coming in to the country, for example as receipts for exports. For the industrialised nations the effect has, by and large, been good: prices paid for imported raw materials and certain manufactured

1. There are exceptions to this: certain staples are low in usable protein, and children need more protein than do adults. The effect of changes from breast to bottle feeding on nutrition — and the role of transnational corporations in promoting this change for economic gain — is a tragic and well documented story. See, for example, the War on Want study by Muller (1974), or the work of the Jelliffes, one of whose papers is reprinted in Abelson (1975).

goods relying on cheap labour have been kept low while export prices for their own capital-intensive manufactures have been kept high. But the effect on the Third World nations has been quite the reverse. They have been forced to sell their raw materials and other exports at scandalously low prices in order to pay for their imports. And the relation between the price they get for their export crops and the price they pay for imported goods has steadily worsened as is shown, for example, by the often quoted banana/tractor ratio: in 1960 3 tons of bananas were enough to buy a tractor; by 1970 it took 11 tons for 1 tractor. Similarly we can take other leading crop and mineral exports and relate them to oil purchases or to interest repayments on debts and get a similarly depressing picture as does *South* each month with fourteen different exports for the 1975-81 period. (On this problem see also ICIDI Ch 9). The poor nations can do little about this situation because they rely so heavily on one or two key exports which the developed nations can stop buying temporarily to force prices down. They would get more money if they processed the goods themselves (e.g. if they exported instant coffee rather than coffee beans) but are again blocked in this development because of the high tariffs which the developed world places on such processed exports. The profit is in the processing and the developed nations keep a tight hold on this lucrative stage of the game.

Whether there is enough statesmanship and true international spirit in the rich countries to recognize that changes in bargaining power and resource pricing (including human labour) are long overdue in the interests of global justice and global stability will determine the character of world politics in the coming generation.

R.J. Barnet & R.E. Muller *Global Reach:
The Power of the Multinational Corporations*
(New York 1974: 210)

The situation is aggravated when the Third World elites use scarce foreign exchange to pay for ostentatious western-style urban projects and luxuries; Gerard Chaliand gives data from French West Africa in the 1960s, for example, which show that the value of imports of alcohol and perfumes was as large as the total value of imports of fertilisers, tractors, agricultural equipment and machine tools combined (in *Partisans* Paris No.29-30 1966: 15-19). Such wastage of foreign exchange is even less acceptable today given the large food imports necessary to offset the lack of home production. Tudge tells us that "Third World food imports . . . doubled between 1955 and 1966 (though the increase has since slowed to around 3.4 percent per year); but in 1955 the Third World paid 996 million US dollars for their food imports, and an estimated 9,000 to 10,000 million US dollars in 1973-4" (1979: 25). In absolute terms the Third World increased its cereal imports from 20 million tons in 1960 to 50 million tons in the early 1970s and to nearly 80 million tons by 1978-9 (ICIDI 1980: 91). The Third World has no bargaining power either in selling or in buying — for the food must be bought, thereby worsening their balance of payments deficits, putting them even more in debt and thus deepening the 'dependency' situation.

5. Food: the ultimate weapon

The increasing food needs of the Third World lead to the final result of dependent development examined here. This, the most ominous, is

NACLA: *Yanqui Dollar* (NY 1971)

> **"For I was hungry and you gave me meat . . ."**
> Matthew 26: 35
>
> The growing dependence of poor food-deficit LDCs
> (less developed countries) on imported grain and the
> continued desire of affluent peoples to increase their
> consumption of animal products promise generally
> strong markets for US grain exports . . . . Moreover,
> ability to provide relief food in periods of shortage or
> famine will enhance US influence in the recipient
> countries, at least for a time.
>
> This dependence is also likely to lead to resentment of
> the US role on the part of the dependent countries.
> Nevertheless, many will find it expedient to accommo-
> date US wishes on a variety of issues.
>
> In a cooler and therefore hungrier world, the US's near-
> monopoly position as food exporter . . . could give the
> US a measure of power it had never had before . . .
> CIA 1974: 34-5, 39
>
> One wonders, in fact, if those who contribute to keeping
> these masses hungry do not know exactly what they are
> doing, since famished, lethargic, diseased people are
> notoriously bad at overthrowing anybody.
> George 1976: 33

the possibility of the rich world using food as the ultimate weapon to
maintain its dominant position. (It could also be used against the
USSR which is a big importer of grain from the USA.) In 1974 the
Central Intelligence Agency of the United States Government (CIA)
published a study entitled "Potential Implications of Trends in World
Population, Food Production, and Climate". It was outspoken about
the benefits which would accrue to the US with its dominant position
in the grain market in an increasingly hungry world: "The world's
increasing dependence on American surpluses portends an increase

in US power and influence, especially vis-a-vis the food-deficit poor countries . . . . In bad years, when the US could not meet the demand for food of most would-be importers, Washington would acquire virtual life and death power over the fate of multitudes of the needy. Without indulging in blackmail in any sense, the US would gain extraordinary political and economic influence" (1974: 2, 40-41). It would seem that this document was intended as a clear threat to Third World nations of what might happen to them if they tried to follow a development path of which the USA disapproved. The example of Chile suggests this: food aid was drastically reduced when Allende's socialist government was elected but resumed when the US-backed military dictatorship toppled Allende and took power. The recent suspending of US aid to the socialist government in Nicaragua is another example (*NACLA Report* May/June 1981). Certainly Earl Butz, a former US Secretary of Agriculture, was quite open in declaring, "Food is a weapon."

Efforts to break out of the cycle of dependence and hunger such as attempts at land reform or gaining higher prices, for example by processing raw materials in the country of origin, are against the economic interests of the transnational companies and developed nations profiting from the present situation who have both the economic and political power to maintain the status quo.

How it affects us: what can we do?

Besides the general effect — that we live in the wealthy nations which benefit from the system — it is easy to find dozens of examples of how this dependency benefits us directly in our day-to-day lives. We drink cheap tea because of low wages paid to the workers on the estates in Sri Lanka. Our meat would be more expensive if it were not for cheap imported feedstuffs. We can buy okra, chillies and green peppers from Kenya, mangoes from Brazil, pineapples from Malaysia and the Ivory Coast, bananas from Ecuador, nectarines from Egypt, carnations from Colombia and so on through a host of different products. These are not necessities and they are being grown on land which is needed by the people in the Third World to grow their own subsistence crops. For us it is a matter of luxuries, for them it can be a matter of life and death.

By changing our diets we can reduce demand for these imports. This should not be viewed as a 'sacrifice' for the poor however. Rather it should be seen firstly as a move towards a more just use of the world's resources and secondly as a step towards freeing ourselves from the pathological over-consumption of food and other goods which big business has encouraged. The Norwegian movement "The

Future in our Hands" starts from this assumption: that as it is the rich countries which are the problem, it is therefore up to the people in these countries (and especially the relatively well-off) to create a new life-style which emphasises human rather than material values. Consuming less does not mean the poor automatically get more. But the rich being less greedy is a necessary *part* of the solution.

The next part of the solution is to educate ourselves: we need information to confront power. Once we begin to see the reasons for hunger we can start putting pressure on the institutions which are responsible. (There are excellent suggestions for further action in George (1976: ch 12) and Lappé & Collins (1977: Ch 48.)

Plantu: *Pauvres chéris* 1978

PART TWO:
THE
THIRD WORLD

We have looked, in general terms, at the reasons for hunger in the world today. To get a better understanding of how these forces operate it is necessary to look more closely at some specific themes and regional examples. In this section, then, we will examine:

(1) agriculture warped by specialisation in Brazil and the Philippines (ch. 5)

(2) the negative effect of applying inappropriate technology in the Third World as illustrated by India (ch.6);

(3) the way inequitable land holding systems and inadequate infra-structure hold back food production, and the difficulty of ensuring that reforms benefit those in need rather than those in power (ch.7);

(4) the way trading patterns established by the Centre keep the Third World poor (ch.8); and

(5) whether aid helps or hinders the poor and whom it does help, taking the example of Bangladesh (ch.9).

A final section (ch.10) will look at alternative strategies, especially those which the people of one country, China, used to break out of the vicious trap of poverty and so eliminate hunger.

5. Export-Oriented Specialisation

Northeast Brazil: Sugar Monoculture

"The enormous strip of *massapé* in the Brazilian Northeast is one of the most fertile areas in the world: it is nine times larger than the cultivable land of Japan which feeds 100 million people. But from our land we get only sugar cane and some subsistence products in quantities well below the needs of the 23 million inhabitants of the region. The reason for this is that the exploitation of these soils, when it takes place, is not designed to provide for the needs of the population but to enrich half-a-dozen large land owners." (Quoted in Michel Bosquet 'Cent mille morts par jour' in *Le Nouvel Observateur* Paris, 21.12.66)

The speaker is Miguel Arraes, former governor of Pernambuco in NE Brazil. The area provides a classic example of one-crop, export-oriented specialisation and the disastrous results it has for the local population. NE Brazil was colonised in the 16th century, the European demand for sugar giving rise to a plantation system worked first by slave labour and later by landless peasants. Once an area of fertile soils and possessing a humid tropical climate suited to agriculture and food production it became a place of hunger. The great sugar estates, the latifundia, bringing profits to the few big land owners, are in sharp contrast to the tiny patches of land, the minifundia, onto which the peasants have been pushed. René Dumont (1965) describes one woman's holding in this region. She grows rice but because the owner will not irrigate the land has to carry all water by hand and therefore gets yields of less than half those she should obtain. The owner takes half the crop as rent while the remaining 336 kg went as follows: 80 kg repaid, at 100% interest, the 40 kg of seed advanced for sowing; 192 kg repaid grain advanced so that she could eat before the harvest; the balance, 64 kg of paddy (40 kg of rice), was her share on which she had to exist for the following year: three-quarters of a kilogram of rice per week. As she observed to Dumont: "I had worked desperately for nothing." Sometimes she can supplement her income by working as a day labourer on the estates, at a rate of about 3p (in the early 1960s) for an eight hour day without food. Yet the Bank of Brazil, judging conditions by the bank accounts of the landlords — swollen by these low wages — rates the area "one of the richest in the north-east".

> . . . sugar cane, an industry that, with lofty indifference, crushed man and cane, reducing everything to bagasse.
>
> de Castro 1970

Food is imported into the area and sold in the estate shops to the workers at inflated prices. The cost of living in Recife is higher than in Rio de Janeiro, black beans cost more than in the luxury resort of Copacabana. A kilo of manioc starch, the staple food of the north-east of Brazil, almost entirely devoid of protein and containing up to 30% cellulose, costs the equivalent of an adult worker's daily wage. An FAO report in 1957 said that in Victoria, near Recife, protein deficiency in children results in a weight loss of about 40%, worse than in Africa; milk is rare and too expensive for the poor; and between 1947 and 1953 there had been a steady fall in the amount of protein available per person.

The latifundia system and sugar monoculture have made of the northeast, in Galeano's words, "A concentration camp for thirty million people" but, as Dumont observes, "those who are responsible for murder by undernourishment are not locked inside, since they are the keepers of the keys". (See Dumont 1965: ch 3, and Galeano 1973: ch 2.)

Recently the ailing sugar industry has received a boost. In 1975, after much research, the Brazilian National Alcohol Energy Programme was established. The aim of the programme is to reduce Brazil's dependence on imported oil by the substitution of ethanol fuel distilled from sugar cane. By this year, 1981, 80% of the cars

> In his case, it was not the drought that had caused his flight from the backlands. He had been able to survive several droughts. It was something much worse that forced him to leave.
>
> "It was the monopoly," said Cosme, "which is a monster far crueler than drought. Besides, the drought comes and goes, and the people it expels can always return to their lands. It is not that way with monopoly. When monopoly comes and establishes itself in a region, it never leaves."
>
> de Casto 1970: 66

In Brazil's Northeast, where men die of old age at twenty-eight, parents feel fortunate when they are able to sell their children into slavery. "My daughter may be used as a prostitute and my son will probably spend the rest of his life working very hard and very long on a Sao Paulo plantation," one father told me when I asked him why he had sold his two children, "but at least they will eat. My other six children were not so fortunate. They stayed here, and they died."

John Gerassi *The Great Fear in Latin America*
(Macmillan, NY 1965: 39)

manufactured by Brazil's biggest car manufacturer, Volkswagen, will be ethanol models. A clean burning, renewable energy seems a positive advance, especially for the car-owning minority. Yet the impact of this swing over from oil to ethanol may have grave consequences for the food situation in Brazil.

The expansion of sugar cane acreage from this petrol substitute means that fuel crops will compete with food crops for land, investment, water, fertiliser and technical services. More people will

The United Fruit Co.

When the trumpet sounded, it was
all prepared on the earth,
the Jehovah parcelled out the earth
to Coca Cola, Inc., Anaconda,
Ford Motors, and other entities:
The Fruit Company, Inc.
reserved for itself the most succulent,
the central coast of my own land,
the delicate waist of America.
It rechristened its territories
as the 'Banana Republics' . . .

Pablo Neruda
in *The Penguin Book of Socialist Verse*
(Harmondsworth 1970)

be squeezed off the land and food prices will increase, badly hitting the poor. More recently, partly to off-set these social costs, manioc has been promoted as a second energy crop in the hope that it will be a cash crop for small farmers who can then buy more nutritious food. It would seem more likely however that this development will simply raise the price of manioc — the last-resort staple of the rural poor. The choice, as one observer put it, is between calories for cars or calories for people. (See Bernton 1981.)

The Philippines: Bitter Fruit

Since the war, agribusiness, controlling production from the farm right through to the supermarket shelves, has become one of the most profitable forms of investment in the Third World. Former US Secretary of Agriculture Orville Freeman, now an advisor to transnational corporations (TNCs), states that "well-run agribusiness projects in some developing countries can return as much as 30 per cent a year on investment . . . and aggressive, imaginative international companies always respond to an opportunity that makes profitable use of their abilities" (George 1976: 162). Certainly profit, not growing food, is what it is all about.

The Philippine islands provide a good example of the giant TNCs at work in league with the country's own elites. The pineapple production of the big firms like Dole and Del Monte used to be concentrated in Hawaii; as workers there became unionised and fought for higher wages, Dole and Del Monte moved their pineapple interests to the Philippines and Thailand where workers get only US$1 a day, leaving thousands unemployed in Hawaii.[1] The growth of the industry has been phenomenal: the Philippines is now the world's largest pineapple exporter and its banana export industry has risen from nothing in the mid-1960s to become the fourth biggest in the world. If the market for these products begins to slacken the TNCs have seafood, frozen fruit and poultry lined up to take over. Three-quarters of the Association of S.E. Asian Nations luxury-food exports go to the affluent Japanese market, the rest to Europe or the USA. The peasants cannot afford to eat what they labour to grow.

The investment necessary for these projects has been encouraged by 'development' institutions such as the World Bank and the Asian Development Bank and by five to twenty-year tax holidays and other financial incentives offered by the host governments. Just as

---

1. We should remember that this doesn't happen only in the Third World: in 1971/2 the giant TNC, Unilever, sacked over 17,000 of their 100,000 staff in Britain in another example of the perfectly rational working of international capitalism (CIS 1975:33)

Vadillo, *Siempre* (Mexico)

The resources of the poor nations provide the basis for the well-being of the rich — and military regimes, often supported from outside, ensure the 'stability' which makes possible this exploitation.

---

important in the Philippines was the state of martial law declared by President Marcos (relaxed in January 1981) and the tight political control of the workers and banning of unions. President Marcos has made much of the supposed land reform in the Philippines to counter criticism of his harsh regime. Yet two-thirds of the country's agricultural land, used by the transnational corporations to grow export crops, was exempted from the reform. Small wonder that only 15,000 of the 1 million peasant tenant farmers supposedly going to benefit from the reform have actually done so; the 3 million landless peasants in the Philippines were not even included in the plan. The *Far Eastern Economic Review* (FEER), 11 July 1980, says that in the Philippine island of Mindanao four major TNCs (Dole, Del Monte, United Fruit and the Japanese trading house Sumitomo) operate 67,000 acres of "choice land which used to be cultivated by occupant-farmers. Thousands of farmers and indigenous minorities have been displaced by the largescale . . . estates": a displacement characterised by strong arm tactics and intimidation according to observers of Del Monte's methods in Mindanao. Small-holders who have refused to lease their land to Del Monte have had cattle driven onto their cultivated land. US companies, according to an American priest, "bulldozed people right off the land. Now they're using aerial sprays harming farm animals and giving people terrible rashes." This priest was subsequently arrested for supporting the peasants (*NACLA Report* Sept 1976: 20).

Yet the TNCs own less and less land outright. Rather they control

There is no reason why free market forces should relate agriculture to nutrition since market exchange reflects the distribution of wealth and income. Any relationship between real and effective demand depends ultimately upon social organization.

. . . in Indonesia there seems to have been an unwarranted haste in committing the Javanese people to new world records of protein deficiency.

Palmer 1972: 84, 62

. . . in this continent [Latin America] of semi-colonies, there die of hunger, of curable diseases or of premature old age some four persons per minute, some 5,500 per day, 2 million per year, some 10 million each five years. These deaths could easily be averted, but nevertheless they continue. Two-thirds of Latin America's population lives briefly, and lives under the constant threat of death. In 15 years this holocaust has brought about twice as many deaths as the First World War . . . and it still rages. Meanwhile there flows from Latin America to the United States a constant torrent of money: some $4,000 per minute, $5 million per day, $2 billion per year, $10 billion each five years. For each thousand dollars which leaves us, one dead body remains. $1,000 per death! that is the price of what is called imperialism. $1,000 PER DEATH, FOUR DEATHS EVERY MINUTE!

Second Declaration of Havana 1962

the land, owned by local grower elites, through contracts and by retaining ownership of processing and marketing. The advantage of this development, as the FEER article remarks, is that it does not tie the company to a fixed investment (land), and "when the resource is exhausted — due to over-intensive cultivation and chemical saturation of the soil — the TNC can easily relocate elsewhere", once again leaving devastation behind them.

In the cases cited above it is clear that while the land *could* grow staple crops to feed the people, it will never be so used under the present system. To those who control the land it makes good economic sense to continue with their luxury crops. Change will come only when those who *need* the food are in a position to grow it; in short when land reform restores control of the land to the peasants.

6. Inappropriate Technology: The Green Revolution

A second factor contributing to hunger in the world today is policies of relying on technical solutions to a problem which is essentially one of social and economic structures. The prime example of such an approach is the so-called 'Green Revolution'.

This was based on Ford and Rockefeller Foundation-funded research into varieties of wheat and rice which would absorb more nutrients (in the shape of oil-based chemical fertilisers) and thus bear heavier kernels which would mean higher yields (hence the term high-yielding varieties or HYVs). Because of their heavier heads they were bred with short stubby stalks (they are also known as 'dwarf' varieties) in contrast to the traditional grains (or the locally improved varieties, LIVs) which have long stalks which lift them above weeds and flood waters. Giving much higher yields *under ideal conditions*, the new 'miracle' seeds, as the salesmen dubbed them, were planted on about 80 million acres of land in the Third World between 1965 and 1973. Suddenly the food crisis was to be solved, and without any uncomfortable social upheaval!

Yet, by themselves, these seeds were *not* more productive than the local varieties. They yielded well only if planted in conjunction with a 'package' which included irrigation, massive doses of artificial fertilisers (three times those required by local varieties), pesticides and fungicides (because they were less resistant to disease than local, naturally adapted varieties) and weed killers (the weeds benefited from the fertiliser and water too!). And as Green Revolution proponent Lester Brown happily pointed out "Only agribusiness firms can supply the new inputs efficiently. This means that the multinational corporation has a vested interest in the agricultural revolution along with the poor countries themselves" (George 1976: 116). That this was not mere coincidence is emphasised by Mooney: "The Green Revolution has been undeniably profitable for agribusiness. By the sixties, agricultural enterprises were in need of a new market to maintain their growth. Bilateral and multilateral aid programmes made expansion into the Third World financially possible. Twenty years later, major agrichemical firms have achieved a world wide distribution system able to market successfully in Asia, Africa and Latin America. The Green Revolution was the vehicle that made all this possible" (1979: 41).

> Erosion of wheat varieties was so fast in the Near East under the advance of the Green Revolution that FAO anticipate the complete loss of the Near East genetic 'centre' by the end of the 1980s.
>
> Mooney 1979: 15

And if the Green Revolution had advantages for western commercial and industrial interests, it also had political advantages: it tied Third World countries to the West by making them more than ever dependent (for supplies and technology) while for the elites of the Third World it offered an increased supply of food to feed their large and restive urban populations. In short, it was hoped, the Green Revolution would stave off a red revolution.

The implications of the increasing control of food production by agribusiness corporations will be discussed in Part Three. In relation to the biology of the Green Revolution three points can be made. Firstly, the food crops we depend on today can all be traced back to nine centres of extreme genetic diversity (called 'Vavilov Centres' after the Russian scientist who pinpointed them) all except one of which are in the Third World. The replacement of innumerable and diverse local strains by the few uniform seed varieties of the Green Revolution is destroying the genetic resources on which humanity is dependent for the maintenance and development of food crops (see Mooney 1979). Secondly, extensive areas of monoculture are open to

> . . . the dangers of monoculture have become obvious. The hybrids are susceptible to virus infestation, which may soon spread to vast areas. Control is then sought with a chemical pesticide, which gets into the food chain and kills off the rice-birds. Rats which eat the dead birds are resistant to the poison, but the black snakes which eat the rats are not so they disappear and the rats multiply wildly. The stalks of the high-yielding variety of rice are short and strong. Rats couldn't climb up the old varieties, which had long weak stalks, but now they devour the rice harvest.
>
> *Manas* March 12 1980: 4

"... the World Bank has replied to the needs of the new phase of capitalist expansion by the industrial nations: replace investment in the agricultural sectors of the metropolitan countries by investment in Third World countries ...." Berthelot & Ravignan 1980: 125

Plantu in *Le Monde diplomatique*

---

grave ecological danger: the epidemic which wiped out the potato crops in Ireland last century illustrates this. And thirdly, natural plant protection systems are destroyed by the cumulative effect of heavy use of nitrogen fertilisers (which produce plants more susceptible to pests) and pesticides (which often eliminate the predators of the pests along with the pests themselves — which in any case gradually develop resistance to the pesticide).

But are these very real costs outweighed nevertheless by the benefits to hungry nations?

The example of India

India illustrates the social and nutritional effects of the Green Revolution. Most HYV planting took place in the already favoured regions of the Punjab and Haryana (wheat) or small pockets of Andhra Pradesh and Tamil Nadu (rice). These regions already had extensive irrigation and high incomes. Haryana, with a per capita income ten times that of West Bengal, spends about twenty times more per capita on irrigation than does Assam (FEA 1976-7: 140). Further, within these already favoured areas, it was only the large farmers who could afford the fertiliser and pesticides which the 'miracle' seeds required. Poor farmers did not have the capital to sink tube-wells for irrigation nor did they have either sufficiently large holdings or the capital for the mechanisation which the new methods called for. Because they matured faster it was possible to grow two crops of the new seeds each year. But in monsoon areas the earlier harvesting time occurred before the dry season and this meant mechanical driers had to be used if the seed was not to sprout or rot. And because the seeds do not reproduce true to kind the farmer cannot save seed for the next planting but must buy new seed every year.

Nor is the fertiliser available even if the small farmers could afford it: "In 1973 India was short of a million tons of fertiliser (calculated at existing levels of consumption — which even for traditional seed varieties is 5 per cent that needed for optimal use)" (FEA 1976-7: 141). The HYV requirements are many times higher.

Ironically, the increased use of HYV wheat and rice has probably had a negative effect on nutrition. Concentration on cereal planting has been at the expense of the protein-rich legumes — the main source of protein for many Third World people. Since the early 1960s legume planting in India has decreased by two and a half million acres. The drop is reflected in the Indian diet: average daily consumption of legumes in India declined 31 per cent between 1956 and 1971 (Lappe & Collins 1977: 142) and the percentage of the rural population affected by serious malnutrition rose from 52% to 70% between 1961 and 1968 (FEA 1976-7: 141).

Bhagavan *et al* (1973) estimate that the package of inputs required per hectare (2½ acres) of HYV rice cost Rupees 1125 in 1971. The national per capita income was only Rupees 600 that year. In the area of their investigation small farmers owning 2 hectares (5 acres) could afford only Rupees 350 per hectare in inputs. The mechanisation needed for the wheat areas means inputs are more expensive and the small farmers can cope even less well. If they borrow to buy the inputs needed for their 'miracle' seeds small farmers have to pay the

Everywhere it is the agricultural labourers, the landless and the near-landless who form the core of rural poverty in Asia . . . Economic prosperity has not simply missed these people; they have been systematically marginalised or proletarianised . . . even in the Punjab where the Green Revolution has raised incomes dramatically, the percentage of the rural population living in poverty has risen.

ILO 1979: 9

extortionate (100%-200%) interest rates of the money lenders as the banks lend only to the big farmers. Unable to pay back these loans small farmers are forced to turn over their land to the money lenders and frequently end up joining the throng of landless peasants, worse off than when they grew the traditional varieties.

The effect of the Green Revolution in worsening the already inequitable land holding pattern by driving small farmers from the land can be seen in the figures for land holdings. In 1951 59% of holdings in India were less than 5 acres (Sharma 1973: 83). But by the early 1970s 75% of holdings were less than 5 acres (and they contained less than one-sixth of the cultivated land; large holdings (over 10 acres) though only 14% of all holdings contained about 65% of the crop land.) The number of agricultural households who owned no land also increased: from 50% to 61% between 1951 and 1964. As the small farmer is bankrupted the land and labour is provided for the large farmer. Between 1961 and 1971 the number of cultivators declined by 22% and by the early 1970s landless labourers accounted for between 30% and 50% of the population in most

---

The industrial nations are increasingly interested in penetrating the agricultures of the underdeveloped countries and have lately found new ways and means to achieve this end. This penetration, even if one assumes that it is not a deliberate strategy to forestall agrarian reforms and other structural changes of benefit to the rural masses, will most certainly have this result . . . . The Green Revolution is far more than the propagation of excellent seeds: it subjects the underdeveloped agri-cultures to an economic and political control which must result from the transfer of technology; and by the same token, it is, and is meant to be, a world-wide counter-reform program . . . . Thus the almost in-credible phenomenon occurs under our very noses that a "program destined to feed the peoples of the world" causes larger unemployment, great poverty, and more hunger in the rural sector.

Ernest Feder *Monthly Review* (N.Y.)
May 1975

states. Between 1961 and 1968, as the Green Revolution spread, the number of people below the poverty line in rural India increased from 38% to 53% (FEA 1976-7: 141).

And India is not alone. In country after country the Green Revolution enriched the better off at the expense of the rural poor, creating what has been termed a 'green bourgeoisie'. Defining the problem as one of production, it focused on a technical solution without confronting the more uncomfortable issue of who controls that production. As a 36 cents-a-day labourer in India knows well: "If you don't own any land, you never get enough to eat, even if the land is producing well" (Lappé & Collins 1977: 134) .

The West has tried to apply its own conceptions of 'development' to the Third World, working through local elites and pretending that the benefits showered on these elites would trickle down to the less fortunate, especially through the wholesale application of Western-inspired and Western-supplied technology. These methods have not produced a single independent and viable economy in the entire Third World — and in fact were not meant to. 'Development' has been the password for imposing a new kind of dependency, for enriching the already rich world and for shaping other societies to meet its commercial and political needs.

George 1976: 17

7. Agrarian Structures

Land Reform

The last two chapters have illustrated the need for land reform if the rural poor are to support themselves. This need is driven home by the statistics of the 1960 World Census of Agriculture which revealed that less than 1% of the total number of holdings (those over 500 acres each) occupied two-thirds of the world's farmland, while 79% of the holdings (which had under 12 acres each) were squeezed onto 7% of the land (Harrison 1980: 45). In the last twenty years the situation has worsened considerably as mechanisation and new 'green revolution' type techniques have profited large landowners and led to evictions and increased rural unemployment. The landless and near-landless constitute 70% to 90% of the rural labour force in many Third World countries (Lappé *et al* 1980: 73, 76). And these figures do not include the millions who migrate to the cities in search of work.[1]

This situation is not only unjust but also inefficient: the World Bank and the FAO, in separate studies, both found that smaller holdings and a lower concentration of ownership produced considerably more per acre and, importantly, employed more people than did large concentrated holdings (Power 1975: 20-1). In Latin America, where FAO estimates that the top 8% of landowners hold 80% of the land, a study of output on small and large farms in Argentina, Brazil, Chile, Columbia, Ecuador and Guatemala, found that output per acre was 3 to 14 times greater on average on the smaller farms than on the larger ones (cited in Power).

Land reform has been attempted in many Third World countries but most of it has been a failure for one of two reasons. Either there was never any real intention that land should change hands — after all it is only the big landowners who have any political pull when it comes to how the land reform laws are drawn up. Or the land quickly reverted

---

1. This situation is similar to that which existed in Britain in the late 19th century when there was repeated agitation because of the 'land hunger' caused by the consolidation of big estates and unjust tenancy laws. Today a new land hunger is emerging as City of London institutions buy up land as a safe investment in a time of economic decline. At the other end of the social scale there has been increasing demand for allotments: during the 1970s the waiting list rose to over 130,000 in England and Wales but plots available fell by 62,000. (See J. Bellini *Rule Brittania: A progress report for Domesday 1986*, Cape, London, 1981: chapters 10 & 11.)

THE NEED FOR LAND REFORM

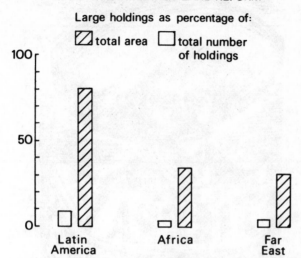

Large holdings as percentage of:

◩ total area ☐ total number of holdings

These graphs indicate that it is not shortage of land but its skewed distribution which accounts for land hunger in the Third World. This manifests itself in the existence, side by side, of large underutilised estates and over-crowded and over-cropped dwarf peasant holdings.

Data: *Ceres* May-June 1981 (For Latin America 'Large holding' is defined as one of over 250 acres; for Africa & the Far East of over 25 acres.)

to the big landowners because no provision was made to transfer to the peasantry either political power or access to other factors of production — credit, technical advice, water, marketing etc.

India gives us an example of such 'false' land reform during the 1950s. Big landowners not only satisfied the legal requirements concerning the maximum land being allowed to any individual by transferring land into the names of relatives but managed at the same time to claim large sums in compensation for the land they had 'lost'. Certain efficient, mechanised or cooperative farms were exempted from the reforms and thus big landholders switched to heavy capital-intensive farming to avoid giving up land and thereby pushed unemployment up. And as a final twist, Sharma cites cases of large holdings which had been divided among relatives being then formed into 'cooperative farming societies' and thus becoming eligible for long term loans and other special treatment by the government! (1973: 91). Similarly we saw how two-thirds of Philippine land (growing export crops for the big transnational agribusiness

"Land must be freed in order to free the human being." Peasant saying quoted by the World Council of Churches, 1981.

(Land American land reform poster)

corporations) was exempted from the land reform in that country. Further it must be stressed that most land reform laws are geared only to small farmers or tenants; the 40% of the rural population which is landless is ignored (ILO 1979). And Baljit Malik (1980) stresses that even where governments theoretically back agrarian reform, peasant efforts aimed at a more just distribution of land and other resources are often in fact savagely suppressed by rich landowners with the connivance of governments.

Clearly if land reform is to succeed it must grow out of a transfer of power to the ordinary people including the landless. The peasants themselves must carry it out so that the laws cannot be evaded and manipulated by the traditional power-holding elites. But if the same situation is not to re-emerge two further important elements must be built into the land reform: a reordering of the agrarian infrastructure and opportunities for co-operation between peasants.

The right of every man to use [material goods] for his own sustenance is prior to every other right of economic import and so is prior to the right of property.

Pope John XXIII
Mater et Magistra 1961

If the need be so manifest and urgent, that it is evident that the present need must be remedied by whatever means be at hand . . . then it is lawful for a man to succour his own needs by means of another's property .

Saint Thomas Aquinas
Summa Theologica

The land belongs to those who work it.
Pope John Paul II
in Recife July 1980

Infrastructure & Co-operation

The poor cannot benefit from land reform unless it is accompanied by a reform of the infrastructure of agricultural development: public works (roads, electricity, irrigation and drainage etc), credit facilities, extension services, crop protection, storage and marketing schemes. In setting up such services it is vital to ensure that the large landowners are not able to monopolise them and thus further aggravate existing inequalities as happened with the Green Revolution. It is also vital that these facilities are not made available only on the condition that self-provisioning subsistence farmers change over to 'modern' export-oriented crops (see Payer 1979). This implies a change in the political power structure so that the peasants control reform or modernisation.

The critical role of credit at low interest rates for the small farmer has been illustrated in earlier sections. Just as important is reform in marketing crops so that middlemen, often the large landowners, cannot dictate low prices to small farmers immediately after the harvest when the peasants have no choice but to sell for whatever they can get. This also implies proper government pricing policies for agricultural goods. Low agricultural prices have robbed the rural areas of capital in order to provide cheap food for city dwellers and

> Agrarian reform cannot avoid the dismantling of power
> structures and therefore, social conflict. Such conflict
> *already* exists. In its most brutal and visible form those
> who benefit from the status quo fight tooth and nail any
> attempts at agrarian reform . . . . Violence and suffering
> become the daily reality for more and more of the
> world's people in countries like the Philippines,
> Nicaragua, Brazil and Chile to name just a few. Less
> visibly, we find growing daily violence against people in
> the form of malnutrition, joblessness and the diseases of
> poverty.
>
> > Rome Declaration Group 12 July 1979
> > (in Whittemore 1981: 48)

cheap raw materials for industrialization and export. An end to this
diversion of wealth from the rural to the urban areas would make
capital available for rural investment and development.

Extension services, the provision of advice by agricultural officers,
are frequently offered in an elitist fashion which undermines rather
than draws out the peasants' own initiative. Often, too, they are
geared only to wealthy farmers and ignore local economic and social
conditions. To succeed they must be operated by the peasants and
small farmers who most need them and they must be tailored to local
geography and traditional agricultural practices as much as to new
technologies. (See Freire (1974) on the destructive elitism of much
extension work.)

But ultimately small farmers with little capital will go to the wall
unless they join together for certain schemes. Irrigation, crop
protection schemes, mechanisation, are all more feasible when
operated jointly by a group of peasants who singly perhaps could not
launch out on solving any particular problem. This will be illustrated
in the section below on China.

Lastly, it is doubtful whether, even with a thorough-going land
reform, all rural unemployment will be absorbed, especially in Asia
(where it is estimated that 35% of the rural labour force is
'superfluous'). No programme aimed at eliminating the hunger
caused by poverty can ignore the necessity of job creation, outside of
agriculture, *in the countryside*. Industrial development, particularly
scattered, small-scale, labour-intensive industries which serve the
agricultural sector and the rural population — e.g. fertiliser works,

agricultural implements factories and repair workshops, processing plants, brick kilns, pottery and clothing workshops etc — is necessary on three counts. Firstly it will help break the dependence of Third World agriculture on the cities and on imports; secondly it will raise the value of exports by at least a measure of processing; and thirdly it will provide both full-time jobs and slack-period part-time jobs.

> To say that rural areas must produce a surplus to finance diversification is to beg the question. Rural areas do produce a surplus now. The trouble is that it is extracted and used to finance luxurious consumption patterns of the rich . . .
>
> Nyerere 1979

8. Trade

The 'international division of labour' rests on the assumption that it is more efficient for some nations to grow certain crops (for which they are 'naturally' advantaged) and for others to produce industrial goods and leave international trade to distribute the products. The rightness of the argument when applied to the food situation depends on whether you measure 'efficiency' in terms of profits for the few or food for the many. The Third World's disadvantaged position in the world trading game has been outlined above. But the way unequal trade keeps the Third World poor, and thus unable to invest in agriculture and industry to eliminate poverty and hunger among its peoples, merits a much closer look.

Part of the aftermath of colonialism is that the world trading system has been determined by the rich industrialised nations who, quite naturally, have set the rules so that they gain all the prizes. Almost totally excluded from the manufactured goods trade by tariffs and

> The consequence for import capacity and economic growth of high dependence on one commodity is clearly shown by the example of Zambia in recent years. There was a boom in copper prices [on which Zambia relies for 97% of its export earnings] from 1972 with the price peaking in April 1974 at $3034 per ton; then it suddenly fell to $1290 before the end of that year. But the prices of imports continued to rise so that the volume of imports Zambia could buy fell by 45 per cent between 1974 and 1975 and the GDP fell by 15 per cent. The gravity of this situation for Zambia is put in perspective when it is contrasted with the 'oil shock' of 1974. This resulted in an increased oil bill for the industrialised countries equivalent to about 2.5 per cent of their GNP. In numerical terms Zambia's shock was six times greater.
>
> ICIDI 1980: 145-6

Vadillo, El Sol de México

quotas, the Third World still relies on primary products for three-quarters of its exports; many Third World countries still depend on just one or two commodities for the bulk of their export earnings, a situation which makes them highly vulnerable to the wild fluctuations of commodity prices.

However, though fluctuating, the trend in primary commodity prices has gone steadily down, relatively, over the past twenty five years: in 1975, among non-oil producing Third World countries, a given quantity of exports bought 21% fewer imports than it did in 1955 (Harrison 1980: 307). Green and Seidman tell us that "the total loss of foreign exchange earnings to the African continent due to falling prices, particularly of agricultural products, *exceeds* all foreign funds which have been invested, loaned or granted to Africa in the two decades since the Second World War" (1968: 40). The resulting balance of payments deficits have sunk the Third World into ever mounting indebtedness; its total debt, already standing at $74.7

billion in 1970, rose to a massive $524 billion by 1981, a situation which means much of its export income is now taken up with repayment of debt.

That these price falls are indeed engineered by the industrialised nations rather than being in any sense dictated by some impartial natural law is suggested by Cavadino: "The prices of foodstuffs exported by *Western* countries in 1966 were 13% above the 1958 level, while the prices of the *same group of products* exported by the devloping countries were 11% lower. For minerals the Western countries' export prices were 5% higher while those of the developing countries were 7% lower (1972: 14).

And just as poverty prevents individuals from buying food so too does it prevent nations. For when we look at world trade figures we find that, despite the pious speeches about fighting world hunger, most of the food is going to the rich, well-fed, Western world: over half the wheat, three-quarters of the corn, three-fifths of the soybeans, nine-tenths of the peanuts and three-quarters of the oilseed cake — much of this to produce meat. When we turn to the trade in meat itself we find that 94.5% (1967-69 average figures) is going to the 'satisfied' world — North America, Europe and Japan; a mere 5.5% to the hungry world. The international fruit and vegetable trade is dominated by the imports of Western Europe and 70% of the world's refrigerated shipping fleet is used to ship bananas to Western Europe and North America! (All figures from Borgstrom 1973: 137-9.)

TRADE – OR PILLAGE

Percentage of selling price going to Third World producer

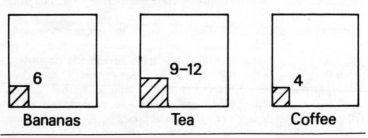

Bananas	Tea	Coffee
6	9–12	4

A marketing system which gives Third World peasants a tiny fraction of the value of the crops they produce is a major factor perpetuating rural poverty in the Third World. (Data from UNCTAD cited by Strahm.)

Clearly, the present trade system is aggravating rather than helping the food crisis. This has led the nations of the Third World to unite in calling for a "New International Economic Order" which would secure reasonable and stable prices for primary commodities, remove the barriers which the West has erected against Third World manufactures, and secure finance for investment in Third World countries without the intolerable conditions which the Western-controlled International Monetary Fund imposes. But although the goals and programme of action they outlined were accepted by the UN General Assembly in May 1974, any action to implement the programme has been completely blocked by the USA, West Germany and Britain. The North will obviously not give up its economic domination of the globe voluntarily and, as *South* (Oct 1980) concludes, "the Third World has no choice but to explore the potential of South-South trade and technological cooperation and to cultivate mutual self-reliance".

9. Aid

Yet, even if the industrialised nations are profiting from trade, surely this is offset by all the aid they send to the Third World? Or is it? In 1978 the aid given by Western nations amounted to only 0.32% of their gross national product. By contrast, the OPEC countries were already giving 3% of their GNP (Harrison 1980: 308; George 1976: 147). The total amount spent on aid ($22.7 billion in 1978, including Communist and Arab funds) is miniscule by comparison to world armaments expenditure: $450 billion a year. For example, the total aid to the whole of Latin America in 1977 amounted to only just over the cost of one nuclear submarine (*Ceres* Nov-Dec 1979: 11).

Also, contrary to the impression given by the 'donors', most aid is not, in fact, 'given' at all. About half of world aid is actually loans and three-quarters of world aid is 'tied' which means the recipient has to spend it on goods provided by the donor country, often at prices much higher than the goods could be bought elsewhere (Cavadino 1972: 17). In other words the 'aid' is actually a subsidy for the donor's manufacturers. Even direct food aid is "in essence little better than a dumping of the surpluses produced by the protectionist policies of Europe and North America" (Harrison 1980: 213-4). It also creates a future market for the donor country's agricultural products.

> The European Community's food aid policy is still dictated by agricultural interests rather than any intention to promote development. It is an inefficient way of distributing European surplus production to the poor countries, associated with high costs, countless mishaps, delays, wranglings over responsibility and bureaucratic obstacles.
>
> Katharina Focke, German M.P. in
> the European Parliament, quoted in
> *South* Dec 1980: 22

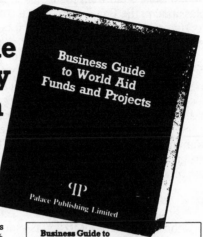
Aid is good business for the wealthy nations.

Nor does the pattern of aid distribution have much relationship to the incidence of poverty and hunger in the world. In 1979 over half the World Bank's aid went to just ten countries, only two of which were classified in the Bank's own 'low income' category. Similarly, of the top ten recipients of US aid only four were 'low income' countries. Almost two-thirds of US aid that year went to just two countries: Israel and Egypt, which suggests the major concern was something other than food for the hungry (Lappé *et al* 1980: 18, 33). In fact, a US National Security Council official stated bluntly that "to give food aid to countries just because people are starving is a pretty weak reason" (George 1976: 210). Perhaps, too, we should remember that military assistance, including the money spent by the US in waging its war on Indochina, is classed as 'aid'. Thus we see that aid and loans are given for reasons of strict political and economic self-interest. Can the money, nevertheless, do any good for the hungry?

The foreign aid programme of the 1960s — as it was in the 1940s and 1950s — is planned and administered to serve the vital interests of the United States. It is a prime instrument of US foreign policy.

Former US Secretary of State
Dean Rusk, 1964

It [the World Bank] is not in the business of redistributing wealth from one set of countries to another. It is not the Robin Hood of the international financial set.

Tom Clausen,
President of the World Bank, January 1982

Only one-quarter of aid funds go to agricultural development and of this quarter the bulk goes to the creation of infrastructure which, if there is no accompanying land reform, means that it goes to the affluent farmers who can make use of it. Of the 13% of World Bank grants to rural development which were allocated to agricultural credit only half are earmarked for small farmers (and the definition of 'small' is very generous) — meaning that half went to large or medium farmers who constitute only 20% of Third World land-holders. The landless, of course, are another matter. (*South* Oct 1980.) Nor does agricultural aid aim at increasing food crops necessarily. In 1974 Togo received $10 million from the World Bank, *all* of which was for the development of cocoa and coffee as cash crops (Dumont & Cohen 1980: 35).

External donations have never been necessary for the
economic development of any country anywhere. Such
donations, moreover, are much more likely to inhibit
development than to promote it. . . .

These gifts have enabled governments to pursue
policies which retard growth and exacerbate poverty,
such as suppressing of productive groups, including
minorities; restriction on the inflow of capital, enter-
prise and skills; and numerous policies which dis-
courage food production.

While aid can do little for development or relief of
poverty, it can relieve immediate shortages. This
enables governments to pursue damaging policies . . .
because the donations temporarily conceal the worst
effects . . .

Aid is *not* given to poor people. It is given to their
rulers — whose policies, including public spending, are
determined by their own personal preferences and
political interests, among which the position of the
common people, let alone the poorest, is apt to have low
priority.

P.T. Bauer & B.S. Yamey
"The case against foreign aid"
Sunday Telegraph 8.2.81

But to see aid at work let us look more closely at one of the major
recipients.

Bangladesh

In the 1970s hundreds of thousands of tons of rice and wheat were
sent to Bangladesh as food aid. Ten percent of this was earmarked for
relief or food-for-work projects (the food in the latter category of aid is
certainly well earned by the recipients) and even of this it was alleged
that much ended up in the black market. But 90% of the food aid went
to the government to sell through its ration system at subsidized
prices. Who got to buy this food? James Boyce and Betsy Hartmann
(who were in Bangladesh from 1974 to 1976) explain that "one-third
of the rationed food grains is allotted to members of the military,
police and civil service. Another third goes to predominantly middle

class ration-card holders in politically sensitive urban areas. The final third is supposed to be sent to the countryside [where 90% of the population live], but it is no secret that the dealers responsible for rationing in the rural areas sell a considerable portion of their stocks on the black market" (in *The Nation*, N.Y. March 4 1978). In fact the sale of food aid provided the repressive government of President Zia with one-fifth of its revenue budget in 1976-7. Thus even well intended aid fails to reach the poor because, as Lappe *et al* point out, it is based on a fundamental fallacy: "that aid can reach the powerless even though channelled through the powerful" (1980: 10).

To turn to non-food aid, a major World Bank project in Bangladesh was to provide 3000 deep tube wells at a cost of $12,000 each. Big enough to irrigate 60 acres of land, these wells are theoretically to be used by cooperatives. But, as we've seen before, such rules can be got around. Boyce and Hartmann quote a foreign expert working on the project: "I no longer ask who is getting the well; I know what the answer will be and I don't want to hear it. One hundred percent of these wells are going to the big boys." The boost which aid thus gives the big farmers is directly responsible for helping push the marginal farmers off the land. An official US study showed that disparities in the countryside were widening and land was being concentrated in ever fewer hands in Bangladesh. Whatever benefits reached the needy they were outweighed by the effects of strengthening the big landlords and propping up a repressive military regime. As Boyce and Hartmann conclude "it is not heartless to propose that at this time perhaps the most we can do for them is to stay out of their way".

Ultimately self-reliance is the only way oppressed people can throw off the constraints binding them and step forward to a life free from poverty and hunger, as China's experience shows.

10. Alternatives

In various parts of the Third World we have examples of different patterns from those outlined above. The state of Kerala in South India shows that the lives of the mass of people can be greatly improved in an extremely poor area if there is a genuine commitment to a more equal distribution of what wealth there is. Kerala is a poor, food-deficit state by comparison to the richer states where the Green Revolution was promoted. Yet we find that infant mortality is 50% lower than in the Punjab (where income per head is almost twice that of Kerala), health standards and life expectancy are higher than in most other states, the adult literacy rate is twice as high as the all-India rate, and the birthrate has declined more sharply than in any other Indian state without any 'hard sell' birth control campaign.

Yet Kerala spends no more on education or health than other states; it does however spend more on schools as opposed to higher education, on rural public health facilities as opposed to measures which will benefit only a wealthy urban group. Many children get free meals at school and there is a public system of fair price shops to see that adults also are adequately nourished. Building on the egalitarian policies of the former royal households such as a fair distribution of land and protection of tenants' rights, the present government has managed to achieve more equality between male and female, rural and urban, rich and poor than is seen in the rest of India (see Chopra, 1981). Kerala has not solved its many problems, especially that of unemployment; it *is* a poor state. Yet it certainly merits consideration for its achievements in the field of social welfare within a country where overall disparities between rich and poor are increasing.

But to see change on a large scale we must turn to the example of China.

China

Before the change of government in 1949, China was, like India, and for similar reasons, a traditional land of famine. Yet by the mid-1970s even formerly hostile American sources were acknowledging China's ability to feed adequately *all* its people.

Mao Zedong recognised that in a country, 85% of whose people

Deep ploughing   Adequate manuring

Irrigation projects   Good seed

Close-planting   Plant protection

Tools reform

Field management

The Eight-point Charter for Agriculture

In many Third World countries where labour is the most plentiful factor for production major progress can be made by careful mobilisation of this labour. The labour-intensive transformation of the Chinese countryside through the techniques illustrated in this series of paper-cuts is an example of this truth.

Source: Buchanan (1970)

were peasants, development had to concentrate on the rural areas. He recognised, too, that the poverty of the Chinese countryside was due not to any shortage of labour or even of land, but to the *underutilisation* of these two factors of production; an underutilisation which was the result of defective social structures, especially the landholding system. The accuracy of this analysis was corroborated by the later work of René Dumont which demonstrated that even in areas of very great land hunger and poverty not all the crop land was being used because the rents demanded by the landlords were higher than the peasants could afford. Only a thorough-going land reform which transferred control over production to the peasants could remedy this situation.

And only such a land redistribution combined with social reorganisation could overcome the other major cause of poverty and hunger: the wastage of human resources through unemployment and underemployment in the countryside. Dumont pointed out as long ago as 1954 that this inefficient use of labour was the main cause of Asia's poverty (1957: 162-3); this was especially true in China where in some areas the peasant could find work for no more than 60 to 70 days a year.

Thus the first step of the new government was a total redistribution of the land, a reform in which the peasants fully participated; through this participation they learned that *they themselves* could change their own circumstances.

But they quickly found that changing land tenure alone did not solve the problem of production. The individual plots were too small to take up all their time (and agricultural work in many parts of China is very seasonal and there was no alternative work for the slack seasons) and also too small for infrastructural improvements. In answer to these problems the peasants began to come together in collective organisations, as the tasks facing them became more complex. In 1958, after several stages of cooperatives, they finally created the commune system. Much more than collective farms, the communes are political, administrative and social units in which the peasants organise agriculture, public works, rural industry, education and welfare services. They consolidated land, labour and capital and were thus able to confront large-scale water conservancy, irrigation and afforestation which were the necessary base for rural development.

For, as in many Third World countries, even more important than land as an underutilised resource was the labour force. Mao saw that the mobilisation of the people was the only basis for development. Public works projects helped eliminate unemployment (and underemployment in the winter) and created new wealth. Terracing effectively increased the amount of land available. Water conservancy — dams, irrigation, drainage — helped reduce the impact of floods and droughts.

Socially the communes made possible a widespread rural health programme which, during the 1950s, effectively eradicated 'the five plagues' — malaria, schistosomiasis, kala azar, filariasis and hookworm. The improvement in health — through a system geared not to a tiny urban elite but to the whole of the rural population — was important in the emergence of a more productive peasantry, as, indeed, was the extension of education.

The rise in farm output and the collective approach meant that investment could be made in diversification of activity in the countryside. China developed and introduced its own high-yielding varieties of rice and wheat before the American-backed Green Revolution got under way (Stavis 1975) and, with improved irrigation, was able to widen both the variety and range of other crops. Pig and poultry rearing, fish farming and dairy production, were all extended.

But the Chinese rural economy "walks on two legs". This means that the improved agriculture was complemented by a widely distributed rural industrialisation. The industry ranges from traditional crafts to quite sophisticated engineering; but an essential component is the maintenance and building of farm machinery and the processing of foodstuffs. This rural industrialisation has been possible not only because of a deliberate policy of decentralisation and the expansion of the supply of electricity but also because of the liberated initiative of the peasants themselves. It is this diversification which helped to wipe out in China the poverty caused by unemployment which, in the Third World today, causes widespread hunger.

Crucial in China's development strategy was the emphasis on self-reliance. Nationally, China relied to a large extent on its own resources and thus broke the pattern of 'dependent development' which hampers most Third World countries. And, within China, organisation and initiative was encouraged to come "from the bottom up" which resulted in the communes being balanced communities, offering scope to the individual's potential, whose level of well being was sufficiently high to help avert the disastrous mass exodus to the cities seen in other Third World countries.

To measure how effectively the people of China solved the problem of hunger a comparison is useful. China started from a situation similar to that of India. By the early 1970s it was estimated that China produced about 75% more grain per person than did India (FEA 1976-7). But the effect for the individual is greater than these figures suggest because in China the distribution of income and food is far more even than in India where the average hides wide disparities between rich and poor. The Chinese showed that control by the people over the allocation of production was no less important than control over the factors of production if a start was to be made in overcoming hunger. (For more details of China's transformation see Aziz 1978 and Buchanan 1970.)

"(Chinese) society has been transformed, poverty all but removed and agricultural production keeping steadily ahead of the growth in population.

The path the Chinese have taken to bring this transformation about is only one possible way to reduce poverty, but it contains many of the features necessary to any attempt to secure the basic needs of all the people."

ILO 1979: 37

The correctness of Mao Zedong's development strategies is perhaps emphasised by recent events in China. The new leadership has taken China along a very different path from that charted by Mao; for example the emphasis on self-reliance has been greatly reduced and imported technology and more capital-intensive forms of development now have greater importance. Disparities between town and countryside, richer and poorer, appear to be growing again and in the last year there have been reports, for the first time since the revolution, that widespread unemployment and hunger have reappeared in China. There may be a lesson in these disquieting reports.

The realities of the 1980s must not ignore China's experience with delinked development strategies and priorities. However, there is also a necessity of looking at China's new eagerness to become part of the existing patterns of political and economic relationships.

Arruda 1980: 2

PART THREE:
AGRICULTURE IN THE INDUSTRIALISED SOCIETIES

Western agriculture claims to be the most efficient in the world and the only answer to solving the problem of hunger in the world today. Yet if we can speak of Chinese development "walking on two legs," we might equally say that agriculture in the industrialised societies "walks on two crutches": 'ghost acreages' and cheap energy. Therefore in this section we will first look at the efficiency of agriculture in developed societies (ch. 11). We will then look at the ecological, political (ch. 12) and social (ch. 13) effects of this form of agriculture. Finally some alternatives to the present system will be outlined (ch. 14).

11. Efficient or Wasteful?

'Ghost Acreages'

In the section on trade we saw that most of the food moving between countries is going to the industrialised societies. Much of this food is used not directly but as animal feedstuffs in the production of meat and eggs in the intensive systems of developed agriculture. Thus the success of, say, Europe in feeding its population is based not on its own agricultural land alone but also on "an added continent, in tilled land more than half as large as its own total of cultivated soils and equal in size to that of South America" (Borgstrom 1974: 111). This extra acreage is needed largely because of the high animal protein diet which we in the industrialised societies have come to believe we need

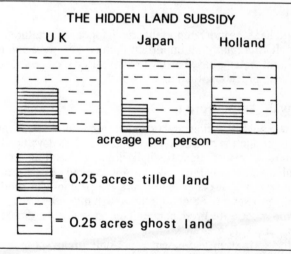

THE HIDDEN LAND SUBSIDY

UK   Japan   Holland

acreage per person

= 0.25 acres tilled land

= 0.25 acres ghost land

The developed societies use far more land to feed their populations than that under cultivation in their own countries. Massive imports of food and feed mean that they are, effectively, utilising not only the land in other countries but also the oceans to supplement their own food production. Thus, for example, the UK has 0.34 acres of tilled land per person but utilises the equivalent of a further 0.98 acres per person through imports and ocean crops. (Data: Borgstrom 1973: 175)

and have a right to. For example, 75% of the world's food fish catch is
eaten in the developed societies, much of it indirectly in the form of
meat from animals fed on fishmeal. Such ocean crops make up about
half of the developed societies' 'ghost acreages', the rest being trade
acreage (i.e. the area of tilled land which would be needed to raise the
food at present acquired by net imports; the concept is Borgstrom's).
The impact of this diversion of food, via animals, to the tables of the
wealthy nations is not only wasteful of food and unjust; it also means
that the developed agricultural system's success rests on enormous
hidden subsidies. Without this crutch our diets would be very different
and our agriculture would seem far less successful.

> Do the Europeans realise that their net importation of
> plant protein through food and feed commodities
> exceeds the total intake of India or that it is one-fifth
> above that of Africa?
>
> Borgstrom 1974: 111

But perhaps the more important crutch for our agriculture is 'cheap'
energy. It is certainly an important factor when we come to ask if
agricultural systems based on the industrialised societies' model have
any chance of feeding the hungry world.

Energy & Agriculture

When we speak of 'efficiency' in agriculture what do we mean? If we
measure production *per person* in agriculture then developed society
agriculture is very efficient (though not as efficient as it claims: in
such calculations only farm workers are counted against production;
to get a true output-per-person figure the people who produce the
tractors, fertiliser and other supplies which make for efficiency, and
those who process the product after it leaves the fields, should also be
counted. See Perelman in Merrill, 1976.)

But this form of measurement is not only irrelevant in a world of
underemployment it is, in effect, a confidence trick, ignoring the
whole purpose of agriculture which is to gain energy for humanity. By
this is meant that the fundamental source of renewable energy on
earth is that synthesised by plants from sunlight; we gain this energy
by eating either plants or the products of other animals which have
eaten those plants. Agriculture harnesses this energy systematically.
In the process, it must use energy (the minimum that can be used is

that represented by the food intake of a person working the land). The true measure of efficiency is thus the amount of energy gained in food as compared to the amount used to produce it. So how much energy does intensive modern agriculture use?

Borgstrom tells us that "when all energy inputs on the farm are added up, many a Western farmer is employing far more energy than his crops collect" (1973a: 218). For example, in 1968, the U.K. agricultural system used 3 to 5 units of energy for every unit it produced on the shop counter (Leach 1975: 29, 35). By contrast East Asian wet rice cultivation gives a 50-fold return for every unit of energy invested (Steinhart & Steinhart 1975: 38-9); 'primitive' New Guinea subsistence agriculture gives a 20-fold return (Dumont & Cohen 1980: 133).

In 'primitive' cultures, 5 to 50 food calories were obtained for each calorie of energy invested . . . . In sharp contrast industrialized food systems require 5 to 10 calories of fuel to obtain 1 food calorie . . . the choices appear to be either less energy intensive food production or famine for many areas of the world.

Steinhart & Steinhart 1975: 39

Two innovations in the agriculture of industrialised societies, basically dating only from the 19th century, account for much of the energy use: mechanisation (including transportation) and the use of artificial fertilisers. Worldwide, these two inputs account for 92% of the commercial energy used in growing food (*Ceres* Nov-Dec 1980: 16). But a true picture of energy use in food production must also include non-farm inputs, e.g. the packaging and processing of food. Leach gives the example of a sliced, wrapped loaf of white bread: "just under 20% of the total energy is consumed in growing the wheat, and all but 3% of the rest is in processing, packing and transport" (1975: 32).

Almost forty years ago Fred Cottrell compared energy use on wet-rice farms in Japan and in Arkansas, USA. In Japan, using traditional methods, it took 90 horsepower hours to cultivate and harvest an acre of rice. In Arkansas, for the same yield of 50 bushels an acre, it took over 800 horsepower hours — and this was just for operating use; it didn't include energy used for producing the tractor and equipment (1955: 138-40). Energy use in modern farming is even higher. We are told by the Center for Economic Alternatives that "US corn requires

ENERGY INPUT–OUTPUT

US Agriculture
overall figure

Indonesian wet–rice
culture

○ = 1 calorie of energy consumed

□ = 1 calorie of food produced

Contrary to popular belief, the developed societies are relatively inefficient agricultural producers, that is, if we measure calorie output in the shape of food against calorie input in the shape of energy.

Data: Steinhart & Steinhart 1975

50 times as much fossil energy as Mexican corn for the same yield" (quoted in *Manas* 21.2.79).

What this all adds up to is that the energy-intensive agricultural systems of the industrialised societies are, contrary to popular belief, highly inefficient energy producers and no model for the Third World in its attempts to solve its hunger problem. The more so because, ironically, as they produce more to meet the demands of a rich minority, they are creating an ever greater *need* amongst the poor: those without the economic power to get their voice heard.

> To feed the entire world with a US type food system, almost 80 percent of the world's annual energy expenditure would be required just for the food system.
>
> Steinhart & Steinhart 1975: 38

But let us look a little more closely at the dimensions and effects of this energy-intensive agricultural system.

Some Effects of Energy-Intensive Agriculture

Apart from machinery and transport the other big energy users in our agricultural system are artificial oil-based fertilisers, especially nitrates, and, to a lesser extent, pesticides.

Until about the middle of the 19th century nearly all the fertiliser used in farming was organic, that is animal manure and plant or 'green' manure. But by 1954, in the USA, 97% of the fertiliser used was artificial (Merrill 1976: 296). The manufacture of artificial fertilisers requires very large amounts of the increasingly expensive fossil fuels. Moreover, chemical fertilisers have far reaching ecological effects. They do not maintain the structure and organic content of the soil as do organic manures; they lessen plants' resistance to disease and pests and thus contribute to higher pesticide usage; and they upset the natural balance of compounds in the biosphere. Over-fertilisation can result in "the accumulation of toxic forms of nitrogen in water supplies and crops" which, in the form of nitrosamines, are carcinogenic (i.e. cancer-causing) (Merrill 1976: 299). Lastly, we may add that the law of diminishing returns applies: Barry Commoner tells us that between 1949 and 1968 total US agricultural production increased by 45% but over the same period annual use of fertiliser nitrogen increased by 648% (1972: 149). Britain's agricultural output per acre increased 50% between 1900 and 1970; its use of nitrogen fertiliser increased 800%, of potassium and phosphorus 300% over the same period (Tudge 1979: 12).

The use of chemical-based pesticides also has serious ecological consequences. They can kill not only the pests but also the predators of those pests leading to a bigger problem than before. Lappé and Collins notes that, compared with thirty years ago, American farmers "use 12 times more pesticides yet the percentage of the crop lost before harvest has almost doubled" (1977: 49).

Many of these pesticides are also highly dangerous to other animals and plants including human beings: the UN's World Health Organisation estimates that half a million people are poisoned by pesticides each year; 5000 of them die. But knowledge of their lethal impact does not stop the use of dozens of these chemicals. DDT is still exported to the Third World by the US manufacturers who are now banned from selling it within their own country. Many more pesticides which are heavily restricted in the US are exported for uncontrolled use in Third World countries: 2, 4, 5-T, for example, one of the herbicides that laid waste Vietnam and which causes birth defects, is still widely used around the world.

Manufacturers who export dangerous pesticides to the Third World claim they are needed in the battle to feed the hungry. Yet most pesticides used in the Third World are applied to export crops. The peasants working in the fields are exposed to poisoning but do not even get any extra food as a result. (See Weir and Schapiro (1981) for a full account of the cynical export of dangerous pesticides to Third World countries.)

> Recipient countries are often unable to stop the hazardous imports [of pesticides banned in the USA]. Western countries do not usually inform developing countries of the hazards of their export products. (A US embassy official admitted to a Congressional investigator from the General Accounting Office that he "did not routinely forward notifications on chemicals not registered in the host country because it may adversely effect US exporting") . . . The heavy trade in pesticides is already coming back to haunt us. Imported foods we eat are often contaminated with carcinogenic pesticides.
>
> Dennis 1979: 16

We have already mentioned the dangerous ecological implications of monoculture and the depletion of the gene pool. A less well known effect of the industrialised food system, with its diet high in animal protein, is the amount of water required to obtain it. Borgstrom tells us that of the total amount of water required (3,500 gallons) to raise the

> Food is thus via man a top-ranking ecological force . . . In his drive for survival, man has created more acres of desert than of new land placed under irrigation. He has pulled down more than half the world's forest cover, thus exposing vast lands to the destructive forces of water and wind. He has destroyed topsoil through excessive cropping on acreages many times larger than he ever built up or created . . . [he cannot] restore the hecatombs of water he has removed from under the ground into the oceans and the atmosphere . . .
>
> Borgstrom 1973: 202, 203

average daily food for one person in the US, 80.5% is used for meat, milk, eggs etc (including that needed to grow the required feedstuffs), 11% for fat and oils, and only 8.5% for plant products (1973: 65). This hardly makes our system suitable for extension to parts of the Third World where water for irrigating plant crops is a precious commodity.

These then, are a few of the ecological costs of a fossil-fuel intensive agriculture. But the political and social costs of the developed world's agriculture are just as important. We turn to these in the next two chapters.

12. Corporate Control of Food

The Developed Societies

One of the biggest changes in the food industry of the developed societies since the Second World War has been increasing vertical integration. By that is meant that one firm controls as many segments as possible of the line from inputs, through food production (on the farm), to processing and marketing. As the Chairman of Del Monte boasts: "We literally begin with the seed and end at the grocer's shelf" (quoted in Hightower 1975: 162). At the same time a few firms are controlling an increasingly large percentage of farms and food commodities. In the mid-1930s there were 6.8 million farms in the USA; by the mid-1970s there were only 2.8 million; and by 1985 it is expected only 1 million will remain (George 1979: 24, 31). While many of these technically remain 'family farms' most are tied into the agribusiness food system through reliance on corporation inputs or marketing or through contracts which regulate what and how they grow. The contract often specifies that the farmers will buy the inputs such as seed and fertiliser from the agribusiness company to whom they will also sell the product. In a monopolistic market they have little choice but to accept the terms dictated. As Hightower comments: "It all adds up to corporate control of the farmer's produce, without having to buy the farm and the farming equipment, and without having to take the risk of production. Those burdens are left to the farm family" (1975: 165). The American Agricultural Marketing Association estimates that by 1985, 75% of American food will be controlled by these integrated food firms.

Just how concentrated the food system has become can be seen by the following statistics which relate to the US where the process is most highly evolved. At the farm input end of the line, four firms control 68% of the petroleum products, 74% of the agricultural chemicals and 80% of the rail transport. Just two firms supply half the hybrid seeds sold and "there are many farming areas where feed must be bought from Ralston Purina or not at all" (Hightower 1975: 140). At the other end of the process Susan George tells us that over 55% of the market is controlled by four or fewer firms (the definition of 'oligopoly' conditions) for *every* major food category in the United States; and in many categories the percentage is far higher (1979: 27).

There are 32,000 food manufacturing firms in the USA but just 50 of them make 75% of the industry's profits (Hightower 1975: 8). The range of 'brands' creates an impression of competition but means nothing; one firm will market under a variety of brand names.

> Let us visit a supermarket in Britain. Take a trolley and fill it, buy the provisions for your family for a week, or a month, and without realising it everything you buy, from baked beans to fish-fingers, orange squash, chicken, margarine, oysters, cheese, sausages, peas, salmon, toothbrushes, razor blades, hairdye, heavy duty detergent, soap, perfume, soup, frozen supper, and ice-cream . . . the list could be extended still further and every item still comes from the same company . . . . More and more people the world over use what one company produces every day of their lives . . . . If you have a television set you can hardly spend a day anywhere in the world without watching and listening to them, for they are the biggest advertisers on earth and spend more money advertising than many governments on the education of their people. Yet you will in all likelihood never hear the firm's name.
>
> Profile of Unilever by G. Tempel
> (quoted in CIS 1975: 6)

Many of these firms are not primarily food firms at all — the biggest farmer in the US is the oil and pipeline conglomerate Tenneco — but have moved into the field for the straightforward reason that there is big money to be made. And those profits come from the consumers: the US Federal Trade Commission found in 1972 that "monopoly power in 13 food industries had cost eaters $2.1 billion more than they should have paid, and that was a conservative estimate" (Hightower 1975: 62). The situation is similar in Britain.

Effectively this control means that a handful of firms now dictates not only what kind of food is grown but also *for whom* it is grown. The criteria on which their decisions are based have nothing to do with nutrition; they are concerned with profit — which means nutrition suffers. In the USA between 1959 and 1970 consumption of milk, fruit and vegetables declined by over 20% while consumption of 'junk food' increased spectacularly: soft drinks by 79%, potato crisps by

85%, to take just two items. And with this change in diet food industry profits increased substantially (George 1976: 167). The biggest profits are to be made by 'adding value' to the crop, i.e. by processing, or, indeed, by creating a product almost totally artificial. In 1974 the U.S. Department of Agriculture stated that "94% of the increase in food prices over the past 20 years was the result of added costs by corporate middlemen" (Hightower 1975: 179). And here in Britain, according to a study by the University of Reading's Centre for Agricultural Strategy, almost half of total expenditure on food is to cover processing and distribution costs.

> Americans are perhaps the only people on earth privileged to buy unbreakable perfectly calibrated, dehydrated, rehydrated parabolic potato chips packed in vacuum-sealed tennis ball cans — at dozens of times the cost of the original, long-forgotten potato.
>
> George 1979: 30

> Orange Plus [Bird's Eye/Unilever] might be considered orange minus by many, since it is imitation orange juice, being diluted with water, sugar, syrup, corn syrup and cotton-seed oil, not to mention gum arabic to give the drink body and sodium carboxymethycellulose to give it vegetable gum. There's more: citric acid is added to give tartness, then potassium phosphate, potassium citrate and calcium phosphate are put in to control the tartness. To give it the 'plus' of its name, vitamins C, A and B1 are added. To give it the 'orange' of its name, artificial flavor and artificial color are added. All that for only 25% more money than it would cost you to buy the same amount of frozen orange juice.
>
> Hightower 1975: 95

This changing of cheap calories into expensive calories, together with the providing of hot-house or tropical crops year round, or the promotion of grain-expensive meat, all mean one thing: luxury food is being produced for the few who can pay for it rather than cheap nutritious food for the many who hunger.

　　It is bad enough that we in the developed societies pay far too much for increasingly artificial food. But when we turn our eyes to the global food situation the impact of business on diets is far more drastic.

Global Reach: An Example

The giant British-Dutch TNC, Unilever, the world's biggest food and soap company, illustrates the spread and impact of agri-capital. Its activities "have a decisive bearing on the distribution and control of the food resources of the world" (CIS 1975: 96). This control stretches right along the line from inputs to consumers. BOCM Silcock, a Unilever company, produces animal feedstuffs. Unilever plantations in Africa and Asia — two-thirds of them under oil palms — produce the raw material for its margarine and soaps. In the UK 1000 British farmers are exclusively contracted to Unilever's Bird's

---

Unilever:

Operates in over 75 countries.
Employs 354,000 people worldwide.
Buys from or sells to two-thirds of humanity.
Has world sales (1980) of £10,152 million.
   (Food accounts for about 53% of sales.)
Markets over 1000 products, none of which carry its name.
The UK half of the company alone has 812 subsidiaries.

Its food companies include: Bird's Eye, Batchelors, Walls, MacFisheries, Liptons, John West, Mattessons.
Margarine & fat brands include: Stork, Blue Band, Echo, Spry, Krona etc.

Its other big interest, also using oils & fats, is detergents and toiletries: Lux, Persil, Radiant, Sunlight, Pears, Vim, Sunsilk, Close-up, Signal, Pepsodent, Elida, Denim and many more.

Sources: CIS 1975;
Unilever Report & Accounts 1980

Eye subsidiary for their total crop. Nordsee, the Unilever fish industry arm, does everything from fish farming and catching fish in their fleet of factory ships, to processing it into fishmeal for animals or fish fingers and frozen fish for human beings, to selling it in their restaurants. The whole UK fishing fleet will, at one time or another, be supplying Unilever. And with their monopoly buying and processing power — they are the biggest importer of fats and edible oils in the world — Unilever's control stretches beyond their actual holdings, in some cases to reduce whole economies or governments to dependent status. Unilever processes, transports, packages, sells. Its Market Research Group will know before you do what you want — and if you don't want it now you will when Unilever advertising has finished its job.

Plantu: *Pauvres chéris* 1978

The expansion of agribusiness into the Third World to meet the demands of the developed societies leaves the local people hungrier than ever.

In the Third World most of Unilever's interests are controlled by the United Africa Company International (UACI). Besides 40 African and Middle Eastern countries, the UACI operates in Latin America, the West Indies and Asia (India, Pakistan, Indonesia, Singapore, Malaysia, the Philippines and Thailand). Essentially the UACI is still a colonial company — exporting raw materials from the Third World and importing manufactured goods (Unilever has a shipping fleet to transport the goods). The impact on nutrition is two-fold. Third World countries are exporting protein in the shape of groundnuts (peanuts), vegetable oils, fish etc which could serve a vital function for their own populations (and tying up land in export-oriented cash crops which might be better used producing staple foods for their own people, e.g. grain).

Hungry people cannot eat that which is exported. Nor are they likely to eat from export earnings or benefit from the so-called development achieved through these export earnings. People will escape from hunger only when policies are pursued that allow them to grow food and to eat the food they grow.

Lappé & Collins 1977: 200

And then the precious foreign exchange so earned is used to import luxury goods including foods — ice cream, sausages, frozen foods — for urban elites who have been educated by advertising into western consumption patterns.

Unilever is just one example; we could just as easily examine one of the big American food corporations. But the same point would emerge: that the purpose of business is to make money. If we are concerned about world hunger then the job of food production should be in the hands of people whose first concern is good nutrition.

Global Control

Traditional agriculture in the Third World (as, indeed, in developed societies) did not buy much in the way of inputs and when the food was grown processed most of it right in the farmer's or peasant's own home. This obviously did not leave much scope for profit-making activities on the part of business. In looking at the technology of the Green Revolution we saw that its promotion created the opportunity for the agribusiness food systems of the developed societies to move into the vast markets of the Third World. They supply inputs such as machinery, fertilisers and seeds; for example Pakistan imported 50 tons of the new GR seeds in 1966-7 but, the very next year, imported 42,000 tons (George 1979: 42). They also control actual production, usually through contracted farming as, for example, in the Philippine pineapple industry. And what is grown tends to be high profit luxury crops which are exported to North America and Europe. These do not feed the Third World and are not even a dependable source of income. Finally they process the food grown, thereby greatly increasing its cost. To own and control technological processes is also a much safer power base than actual land ownership: technology cannot be expropriated or nationalised.

An ominous new trend is the expansion of meat production in the Third World, utilising both land and grain which could be better used; a trend encouraged by investment by such 'development' bodies as the World Bank. In Latin America the meat industry has already taken millions of acres of land out of crop production and the trend is continuing; at the same time nearly all Latin American countries have to import increasing amounts of staple foods (Feder 1980). And in Africa, Susan George describes irrigated ranching in the Sahel in areas where people were starving to death (1976).

> . . . increased beef cattle and meat production in the Third World represents a far greater direct, immediate, and long-run danger to nutrition in the Third World (not only its protein intakes) than the Green Revolution, and an enormous additional threat to the survival of the peasantry. It is by any criterion — except that of the improved diet of the rich industrial nations, and that of the superprofits from the superexploitation of resources in the underdeveloped agricultures — an odious development under the conditions under which it takes place.
>
> Feder: 1980: 464

Land which should be controlled by the people who live and work on it, growing food for local people, is instead being used for profitable investment by agribusiness and small elite groups; its produce being sold to those who can pay.

But the TNCs are also penetrating Third World societies at the final end of the food chain: through massive advertising campaigns they are able to change the tastes of Third World people, usually by emphasising that the new food is more 'modern', more 'with it', than the traditional, much cheaper and usually more nutritious diet. Thus bread made from American wheat becomes more fashionable than rice; powdered milk replaces breast feeding. But if peasants or slum-dwellers want to join the Pepsi-generation they can do so only by cutting down expenditure somewhere else — which often means basic foodstuffs get sacrificed.

> The result of teaching the people that their traditional foods are somehow inferior is what one nutritionist has called 'commerciogenic malnutrition'.
>
> George 1976: 169

The TNCs already control over 30% of world food production (WCC *Sharing* Aug 1981: 8). What they are shaping has been termed a 'global farm' to serve a 'global supermarket' where at all stages of the game they are in control. The extent of this control can be

indicated by just one product — and this is not a luxury but an essential — wheat. Hightower notes that "six multinational grain corporations — Cargill, Continental, Bunge, Archer-Daniels-Midland, Dreyfus, Peavey & Cook — handle 90% of all the grain shipped in the entire world. Cargill and Continental alone split half the market" (1975: 153). This gives them, literally, control over who eats.

Seeds of Profit? Seeds of Hunger?

A particularly dangerous aspect of corporate control is their interest in seeds. The political (and ecological) implications of this have been outlined by P.R. Mooney in his important book *Seeds of the Earth: A Private or Public Resource?* The account given here is based on his work.

In 1961 the principle of 'plant breeders' rights' (PBR), which give private breeders the equivalent of patents (and thus royalty payments) on their newly developed varieties was established. Recognition of the profits now possible brought non-seed TNCs rushing in. Here in Britain, Rank Hovis McDougall, to name one, has acquired over 100 seed companies. This movement of business into seeds means that, as in other stages of the food industry, seeds are now being controlled and developed for profit rather than for reasons of good nutrition. One result is varieties being developed which use more chemicals — the seed market is dominated by companies with agri-*chemical* interests like Ciba-Geigy or Royal Dutch Shell. Thus what should be political decisions — about how best to eliminate hunger —become instead economic decisions about how to increase profits.

In the section on the Green Revolution we looked at the ecological implications of destroying the genetic base on which we rely for all plant foods. To counteract the elimination of traditional varieties gene 'banks' have been established to protect the world's genetic resources. But this is a highly vulnerable answer to the problem. Mooney tells us that the National Seed Storage Laboratory in Colorado —"the world's storehouse for many major crops" — is sited between one of the largest munitions plants in the USA and a nuclear reactor. It is very much a case of putting all your eggs in one basket. For Third World nations, where the great genetic resource 'pools' are located, it is even worse: they are being asked to put *their* eggs in someone *else's* basket! The big corporations are also establishing their own collections of genetic materials; United Brands, for example, holds two-thirds of the world's banana germ plasm. Such corporation gene banks move control one step further away: from governments, at least theoretically answerable to the people, to businesses with no such accountability.

On the marketing side it becomes once again a question not of availability but of ability to pay: the poor lose out. No one should be surprised that commercial firms put profit before people: that, after all, is why they exist. Together with the political elites who both serve and use them they are simply looking after their own interests. But those are *not* the interests of the majority of people whether they be housewives in the UK or the hungry of the Third World.

13. The Social Impact of Capital-Intensive Agriculture

We will look at three aspects of the modern food industry under this heading: ethical, health, and social.

Factory Farming

Intensive animal rearing, or factory farming, is the method by which most of the pork, chicken, turkey, veal, eggs and, to a lesser extent, beef we eat is produced. In this system the animal is reduced to being merely a machine by which saleable food is produced. To this end the animals are reared in grossly crowded conditions where any exercise is impossible, often in almost total darkness. They are fed artificial diets which are deficient in nutrients (veal calves are fed a milk substitute diet, deficient in iron and vitamins, to produce the anaemic white flesh the public is supposed to demand) and full of hormones, antibiotics and other chemicals to encourage growth and stave off the diseases inevitable with such rearing practices. (According to a BBC Radio 4 news item on 10.4.81, 80% of chickens in Britain have salmonella.)

> . . . A few pigs have died from unexplained reasons which might be due to the stress conditions associated with high density stocking. These deaths in no way nullify the extra return obtained from the higher total output.
>
> *Farmer & Stockbreeder* 22.1.63
>
> I think the test of a 'sweat-box' is whether or not it pays. If your pigs are healthy then it's not a worthwhile proposition.
>
> Dr K.C. Sellers, director of the
> Animal Health Trust's farm livestock
> research centre
> quoted by Harrison 1964: 95, 97

The end result is a tasteless product full of harmful residues and with less nutrient value than traditionally produced food. For example, battery produced eggs are deficient in vitamins and minerals by comparison with free range eggs (Harrison 1964: 137-141).

> ... The industry which has conquered the pallid yolk resulting from intensive laying (by the introduction of certain dyes into feed) is now experimenting with a 'chicken taste' extract to meet the criticisms that intensive rearing leads to tasteless meat.
>
> *Financial Times* 11 Oct 1962
> in Harrison 1964: 136

It is this intensive production to meet the commercially created demand for a high animal-protein diet which uses the vast amounts of animal feedstuffs which the developed societies import. Both the Third World and the industrialised societies suffer from such a system: in the Third World it is directly responsible for malnutrition because it uses grain desperately needed by Third World peoples; in the industrialised societies it affects the health of the population through overconsumption and build-up in the body of residues of such substances as antibiotics.

The cruelty it involves is allowed, indeed encouraged, by the hypocrisy not only of farmers and consumers but also of legislation. For example, the 1954 Protection of Birds Act made it an offence to confine birds in a cage insufficiently large to allow them to stretch their wings, but it specifically excluded poultry from the ruling. Yet, continuing with the example of poultry, this cruelty, while making for easier management, is not even economically necessary. Ruth Harrison cites Denmark which has legally abolished battery cages while remaining one of the biggest egg producers in the world. It "has made a system of free range, or deep litter with access to free range in good weather, an economic and flourishing industry" (1964: 156). And in 1980 a German court ruled that the cruelty involved in battery hen production was unacceptable and in future might be punishable under law (*Development Forum* Sept 1980: 10).

But perhaps out of sheer self-interest we should have second thoughts about this cornering and processing by these unnecessarily cruel techniques of so much of the world's cereals for as Harrison says "the degradation of the animal in the appalling ways it is now made to eke out its existence must have an impact on self-respect, and ultimately on man's treatment of man" (1964: 7-8).

> ... in the universal game of business, everything under the sun, animal, vegetable, or mineral, can be manipulated by certain players for profit ... [This view] originated in an attitude towards *material* things, which then evolved into a like attitude towards *people*.
>
> Hunter 1970: 176

And, indeed, such an impact can already be seen in the living and working conditions of the migrant labourers utilised for certain parts of the agricultural system where mechanisation is either impossible or dearer than the wage levels of this class of worker. To the food

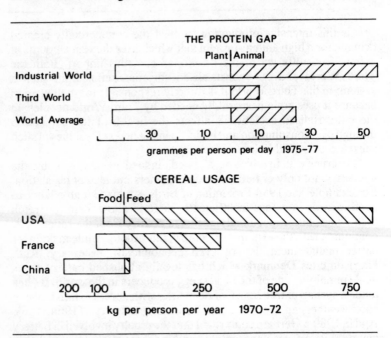

Not only does the industrial world consume far more protein than the Third World, but it obtains the extra almost completely from animal rather than plant sources. The cost of this consumption of animal protein in terms of cereal wastage is seen in the bottom graph. Because animal protein takes so much cereal to produce (see p. 34) the average citizen of the USA is consuming almost 1000 kg of grain a year, compared to an average of less than 200 kg in the Third World. (Data: Protein Gap: *Ceres* March-April 1980 p.5; Cereal Usage: Strahm 1975: 78)

industry they are, like the animals in the intensive units, no more than an input in the production of profit, via food. (See, for example, *NACLA Report* Nov-Dec 1977 on migrant labour in US agriculture.)

The Impact on Health

We have already mentioned the carcinogenic effects of nitrites and the health problem caused by pesticide, antibiotic and hormone residues passing up the food chain to human beings. But the problem continues after the food leaves the farm. A total of 3000 additives were going into food processed in Britain (3890 in the USA) by 1973. In an article titled "Should modern food carry a government health warning?", James Thomson tells us that "the average Briton consumed 1.5 lb of additives in 1955, but this had risen . . . to 2.8 lb by 1970 and [was] estimated to reach 3.2 lb [by 1975]." The average American consumes 9 lb of additives a year, "equivalent to thirty-six aspirin-sized tablets every day"! *(World Medicine*, 24 Sept 1975: 74-5). Half the additives are purely cosmetic; some, like the carcinogenic nitrites added to cooked meats, are preservatives; a few are nutrients, like the vitamin B1 added to white bread to replace some of that extracted from the wheat in refining (most of the other vitamins and minerals are not replaced; the bran and wheat germ removed are sold separately at an inflated price). (For a fuller discussion of the problem see James Turner's *The Chemical Feast*, New York 1970.)

> It is one of the miracles of science and hygiene that the germs that used to be in our food have been replaced by poisons.
>
> Berry 1977: 4

The over-refining of food and subsequent lack of roughage in the diet also contributes to that almost universal problem in the western world — constipation — as well as to diverticulitis (a disease of the intestines) and cancer of the colon. A low fibre diet, high in refined carbohydrate and sugar, also promotes obesity and is a major contributing factor to maturity onset diabetes. Trowell (1974) tells us that these diseases were "both rare in Europe until the eighteenth century." The link with diabetes is emphasised by the fact that deaths from this disease fell sharply during the 1942-52 period when high fibre flour was compulsory in Britain (Trowell 1974: 165). Robert Waller explores the issues further in *Just Consequences* (London 1971) which "suggests that there is a new pattern of diseases in Western civilisation" related to nutrition.

The poor eat 56 per cent less fruit per head than the rich, 19 per cent less fresh green vegetables, 28 per cent less cheese, 21 per cent less milk, 31 per cent less carcase meat, 8 per cent less fat. To make up for this the poor eat 57 per cent more potatoes, 33 per cent more cereal products (mainly bread), 32 per cent more sugar. "The rich" (income group A1) covers people who in 1974 were earning £5000 a year or more. "The poor" (income group D1) covers those earning £1200 or less in 1974, but excludes old-age pensioners and households without income earners. Figures are eleven year averages, 1964-75 inclusive, from the National Food Survey.

Wilkinson 1976: 567

But more important than the health problems of an overfed society is the obscenity, in a world where 15 million children alone die each year from malnutrition, of a problem of over-eating big enough to spawn a whole slimming industry; big enough to persuade the West Germans, just one example, to spend 5 billion DM (about £1 billion) in 1979 in their fight against obesity (Dumont & Mottin 1980: 255).

In terms of health here in Britain we find the same factors at work as in the Third World: what we eat depends on income rather than

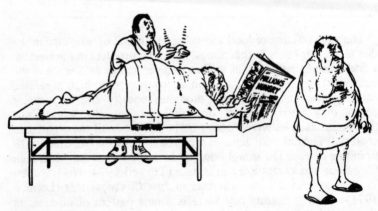

Vadillo — *Siempre,* Mexico

availability of food. The significance of this is that "whether one looks at the relative or absolute size of the gap between the death rates of upper and lower social classes it is two or three times as large now as it was in the early 1930s" and the "nation's diet is the most important single influence on the death rate" (Wilkinson 1976: 567, 568). Despite our 'efficient' food industry poor people are increasingly not getting the food they need and are dying earlier than the rich because of this. Wilkinson notes that income overrides education in diet patterns. The situation is no better in the United States as the quotation below shows.

Millions of Americans are handicapped by hunger and malnutrition — their bodies weak and subject to disease, their minds crippled and performing at a level far below their original potential . . . Hunger is a reality for 15 million hard-core poor, and another 10 million stand in need of some food assistance.

Senator E.F. Hollings in
The Nation (New York) 26.4.1971

As in the Third World the problem is unemployment, poverty, *access* to food, and thus a problem of the ordering of society.

The Effect on Society

They [the machines] promise everything. Look at their colours — blue, red, bright green: they promise the world!
He walked to the door. False promises! He shouted the two words out very loud . . . .
Do you know what those machines are for?
They plough, they turn hay, they spread dung, they milk — it depends, answered Nicole.
There's one job they all do.
He looked into her eyes with the utmost seriousness. . . . . .
Their job is to wipe us out.

Berger 1979: 78

Until well into the 19th century Western Europe was still — like the Third World today — a dominantly rural society. Farming was not merely the work of millions of peasants and the craftsmen who backed them up but the way of life of close-knit, small-scale

> The new agriculture is not calling for farmers . . . . It is calling for the profit-sensitive executives of giant corporations.
>
> Hightower 1975: 39

communities. Increasingly, this century, people have been leaving the land. An ILO report tells us that millions of farmers are leaving the fields of the industrialised world every year: to be precise, 60 million between 1950 and 1970; and it is estimated another 60 million will have left by the year 2000 (*Development Forum* Jan-Feb 1979: 10).

They are being driven off because they don't have the money to compete with the extremely capital-intensive industry which is farming today. They are being replaced by machines. Wendell Berry (1977: 59) quotes two articles which show us where industrialised farming is heading. In the first a US Department of Agriculture official is speaking:

> Fields will be larger, with fewer trees, hedges, and roadways. Machines will be bigger and more powerful . . . . They'll be automated, even radio-controlled, with closed circuit TV to let an operator sitting on a front porch monitor what is going on . . . .
>
> Weather control may tame hailstorm and tornado dangers . . . . Atomic energy may supply power to level hills or provide irrigation from the sea. (*National Geographic* Feb 1970)

The second article (from *The American Farmer* Oct 1974) takes us even further:

> Livestock will be housed (and products processed) in a 15-story, 150' x 200' building. It will also contain power facilities, administrative head-quarters, veterinary facilities, repair shops, refrigeration and packaging units, storage, research labs, water and waste treatment facilities. At capacity, the high-rise building will house 2,500 feeder cattle, 600 cow-calf units, 500 dairy cattle, 2,500 sheep, 6,750 finishing hogs, space for 150 sows and litters, 1,000 turkeys, and 15,000 chickens.
>
> Crops will be grown year around under plastic covers that provide precise climate control in three circular fields each a mile in diameter. At any given time, regardless of weather, one field or crop will be in the planting stage, another in the growing stage, and the third in the harvesting stage.

The tone of both articles is unquestioning, even exultant; they describe an industrialised, scientific agriculture, frightening in its *hubris* but perhaps most notable for the almost total lack of people involved in it.

But this flight from the land, this "forced migration of people greater than any in history" as Wendell Berry puts it, *should* be questioned. For as it occurs, agricultural skills vital to the survival of humanity are being lost. Today's farmers are older and their children have left for the city. When our present high-energy agriculture is no longer sustainable (let alone in the event of a major war with all its implications) we may need these skills again. Even in times of economic recession the social role of small farms is important. During the depression of the 1930s a large percentage of Americans could turn to "friends or relatives on farms that could operate on a self-sufficient basis during lean periods" (Todd in Merrill 1976: 236). We no longer have this buffer.

Such a migration is also a complete break with both the centuries of our own past and the accumulated wisdom of most other cultures which see the land and the people as inseparable, which see the land as the very foundation of human civilisation. Only in the last decade or so have we become aware of the scale of the destruction involved in both human and ecological terms (see Shoard 1980).

The Vision of the Other North Americans . . .

The Cherokee word for land is 'Eloheh'. That same word also means history, culture, and religion. We have no history and no culture if we have no land for them to come from. We cannot think of ourselves as existing without existing directly in the land. Land for us is not property, or even a place to build a house or plant crops. It is something truly sacred in the most profound sense, and it is part of ourselves.

Jimmie Durham in *IFDA Dossier* 6,
April 1979

Have we thought sufficiently of the results of the increasing divorce of humankind from the land, from the natural rhythms of the universe? Have we pondered this while looking at the social disintegration of the western world? This does not imply any sentimentalised view of the past; many agricultural labourers worked long hard hours and lived in conditions of extreme poverty. Change was needed; but whether today's unemployment and poverty in urban slums is a step forward is questionable.

We have had the temerity to deliberately destroy the basis of our culture in a few short years without having any real vision of where the new society we were creating was going: 'progress' was good — but we forgot to ask for whom? and towards what? Is our new pattern as unsustainable in human terms as it is in ecological terms? The choice between exploitation of, and participation in, nature should be too important a choice to be left with the experts.

> Men are made of what is made,
> The meat, the drink, the life, the corn,
> Laid up by them, in them reborn,
> And self-begotten cycles close
> About our way; indigenous art
> And simple spells make unafraid
> The haunted labyrinths of the heart . . .

Edwin Muir, from 'The Island'
Selected Poems (Faber, London, 1965)

14. Alternatives

We have argued that the modern agriculture of the industrialised societies is too resource-expensive, too unsustainable ecologically, too socially destructive, to be a pattern for the future. If this is so, are there alternatives? The answer, most certainly, is yes.

What happens if you stop using chemicals? We have seen that increased use of chemical fertilisers and pesticides brings sharply diminishing returns. And in fact we do not need to speculate about the results of organic farming. The Center for the Biology of Natural Systems (CBNS) has done research into "the production, economic returns and energy intensiveness of Corn Belt farms that do and do not use inorganic fertilisers and pesticides." They found that the organic farms produced crops at a slightly lower (but not statistically significant) overall level but, because of lower costs, were at least as profitable per acre (to use the economist's measure of success) as the conventional high-energy farms. But most important they found that "the conventional sample used an average of almost three times as much energy as the organic sample to produce $1 worth of crops" (CBNS 1975: 47; 1976). Here in Britain we have the example of the Mayall's farm in Shropshire. They began growing their crops on an organic farming system in 1949. With over 1000 acres they are highly successful farmers hardly able to keep up with the increasing demand for their cereals.

Or we can turn to the example of the Amish Mennonite farming communities in North America. Intensely religious, the Amish farm as they did when they came to North America in the 17th century, without tractors, cars or electricity but with exquisite traditional husbandry. And they do it successfully: their land is healthy, they are economically sound and their communities thrive (there are 460,000 Mennonites in the world, the greatest concentration in North America). Wendell Berry gives a detailed account of their methods and then concludes: "since the Amish are manifestly excellent farmers, and are so complexly successful in other ways, one wonders why they have been ignored by the officials and the scholars of agriculture — especially since their technology and methods are so well suited to land not even farmable by orthodox methods and to farmers not able to survive in the orthodox economy. I have been able to think of only two answers, aside from the conventional contempt for anything small: first, the Amish are a thrifty people, hence poor consumers of 'purchased inputs' from the 'agribusiness' industries; and second, they are living disproof of some of the fundamental assumptions of the orthodox" (1977: 216-7).

And we know from the broader studies of the World Bank and FAO, cited in the section on land reform, that smaller, less capital-intensive holdings not only employ more people but are more productive per acre than large concentrated holdings.

Some specific steps by which farming could be made less energy expensive are suggested below:

1. Machinery should be scaled down to a level appropriate for the job. In Third World countries where the biggest resource is under-utilised labour it makes no sense to use machinery to displace labour. It can, however, make sense to use machinery to save time, for example, to get land cultivated quickly so that a second or third crop can be planted.

2. More use can be made of natural manures including human excreta suitably treated. The Chinese example is well known but California's State Architect, Sim van der Ryn, argued that such a policy has as much potential in a highly industrialised society. The manure produced in intensive animal rearing systems creates a pollution problem in many parts of the USA. Wendell Berry cites this as the perfect example of taking a solution (manure for fertiliser) and dividing it neatly into two problems (pollution and the need for expensive chemical fertilisers). The production of methane from manure has potential for much wider application; it would help solve the problem of many peasants who at present must burn dried manure as fuel. More extensive use of sun, wind or water power (for example in pumping water or processing grain) also has potential. We should remember that at the time of the Domesday survey (1086) there were between 5000 and 6000 water mills in Britain; and countless windmills dotted the countryside from their introduction in the 12th century up to the late 19th century.

3. Weed control is more economically carried out by mechanical cultivation such as the use of rotary hoes. In pest control there is great scope for more biological control, such as the introduction of sterile males or natural predators. Where pesticides are used, hand applic-ation to specific areas is preferable to blanket usage.

4. Beyond the farm the energy-expensive processing, transportation and packaging of food presents an area of enormous potential energy savings. For example, in 1978, 6 million gallons of fuel were used to transport lettuce and other vegetables from California to New York (*IFDA Dossier* 19, Sept/Oct 1980: 107). This is ecologically absurd.

TWO WAYS TO INCREASE FERTILISER PRODUCTION

Western technology	Appropriate technology

1 big fertiliser factory in city	Small bio-gas fertiliser plants for 26,000 villages

Total cost

$ 140 million	$ 125 million

Cost of imports

$ 70 million	Nil

Jobs created

1000	130,750
♦	

Energy consumed	Energy generated
100,000 MWh/yr	6,000,000 MWh/yr

Fertiliser produced

230,000 tonnes	230,000 tonnes

For countries starved of capital and facing major problems of un- and under-employment in the rural sector, the western model of development is inappropriate. (Redrawn from Strahm 1975: 90)

5. It follows from 4 that in the developed societies there should be a return, where possible, to food being produced where it is to be eaten. Learning what foods we ourselves, and our local area, can produce may deprive us of year-round salads or tasteless imported fruits in winter. But on the other hand we might be able to regain a little of the control over food resources which we have relinquished to remote agribusiness firms (see e.g., Joan Dye Gussow in *Ceres* May-June 1981).

On the question of ways to increase available food, the developed societies could, with benefit to themselves, cut drastically the amount of animal protein they consume, thus freeing grain and other foods

WHICH CROP

**0.25 acres provides food
for 1 person for:**

**549
days**

**217
days**

**19
days**

Meat   Grain   Soya

The inefficiency of livestock as food producers is illustrated by this diagram. The same area of land will feed a person almost 30 times longer if planted to soya beans rather than if used for livestock.

However, in spite of the potential value of soya as a human food, 97% of the world's crop is used as either animal feed or as the raw material for the synthetic fibre industry. (Redrawn from Strahm 1975: 94)

used as feedstuffs. The use of less conventional foods, especially protein-rich plants, could be extended. At present only 200 or 300 of the 3000 or so edible plants on the earth are regularly utilised(Dumont & Cohen 1980: 191) and 80% of the world's food comes from just three grains — wheat, rice and maize — and three tubers — potato, yams and cassava (Borgstrom 1973: 10). Research into traditional plants, including tree crops, aimed at producing better strains for marginal areas is also necessary. Fish farming could be extended but its usefulness depends on the fish being used for human consumption rather than as animal feed. On the broader scale, Chonchol (1979a) outlines the essential components of an alternative development strategy which emphasises the rural sector as opposed to the usual urban-based strategies which leave the mass of people poorer (and hungrier) than ever.

This section is very brief deliberately because there is no lack of knowledge of what can and should be done; what *is* lacking is the political will. The most sophisticated technical modifications will only reinforce the inequalities which cause hunger if there is no change in the balance of power between and within nations.

> The harsh reality is that the world elite have convened here to stalk the progress of the rural masses, not to seek ways to alleviate their sorry plight.
>
> The Lesotho Agriculture Minister speaking of the World Conference on Agrarian Reform & Development 1979

Vadillo, *Siempre* (Mexico)

If present trends continue, the world in 2000 will be more crowded, more polluted, less stable ecologically, and more vulnerable to disruption than the world we live in now . . . .

For hundreds of millions of the desperately poor, the outlook for food and other necessities of life will be no better. For many it will be worse . . . *unless the nations of the world act decisively to alter current trends.*

This, in essence, is the picture emerging from the U.S. Government's projections of probable changes in world population, resources, and environment by the end of the century, as presented in the Global 2000 Study.

Not Man Apart Sept 1980: 4
(emphasis added)

To recognize the right of these peasants and the unemployed in the towns to food and to life is to engage in a struggle against everything that limits this right, i.e. against the acquisitive instinct of those who already have and want still more, at national and international level . . . . It is not possible to recognize the right to food and at the same time promote export crops that subsidize, in the Third World, the luxuries of a minority, and finance the purchase of lethal weapons whose production supports the prosperity of the industrialized countries.

Spitz 1981: 30

Conclusion

People don't make themselves poor, they are made poor. The problem of poverty is not a problem of the poor, it is a problem of the rich, a problem of the system which creates poverty.

South editorial, June 1981

At the start of this essay we asked the question: "Hunger — why does it happen?"

We have seen that the economies of today's 'underdeveloped' countries were misshaped by colonialism to suit the needs of the economies of the Centre. We can see the extension of this today in the results of modern agricultural systems whose capital-intensive character actually *increases* hunger by turning people off the land and gearing agriculture to the profitable food and raw material demands of the Centre rather than to the needs of the Third World. The cash-crop policies which dominate so many Third World agricultures are directly responsible for starvation. And modern Green Revolution-type agriculture increases the dependence of the Third World as, indeed, it is intended to: a central reason for its promotion is the creation of new markets for the technology of the Centre (from whom most of the inputs must be imported: oil, fertiliser, machinery, even seed).

In short, throughout the Third World much agricultural development, (like Coca Cola and Mercedes), has been imported from the West and is largely irrelevant to the needs of the people — when not actually in conflict with them. The essentials of a rational agriculture geared to feeding people are simply outside of and opposed to the workings of the international economic system devised and dominated by the North; a system designed to develop the North by using the resources of the South. Dependent societies do not develop because it it not their role to do so. If they want to develop they have to break out of the system and follow an autonomous path of development with fulfilment of their own needs as the central goal. They must break with the countries which have dominated events for so long and re-enter history on their own terms.

An essential link which must be broken in this process is the role of the foreign-educated, externally-oriented elites. These elites are bearers of an alien technocratic civilisation; their links are with the

elites of the Centre rather than with their own people; they are part of
the international economic system which functions to ensure growth
at the Centre at the expense of the Periphery. Their policies and
priorities, the consumption patterns they introduce, are geared to
meet the Centre's needs and not those of their own people: to produce
for the Centre, to buy the Centre's goods.

None of the above is to claim that agricultural production must not
be raised, that modernisation must not take place. Indeed, it must. But
it must be done as part of a policy geared to the needs of *all* the people,
determined and carried out *by* the people, and this will call for a total
restructuring of society. Piecemeal 'improvements' leave the real
problems — the social and economic inequalities, the concentration
of power in the hands of a small elite — untouched.

If we take the example of India we see this very clearly. Undoubted-
ly Indian agriculture has made great improvements in recent years.
The country has increased its irrigated area by 50% and produces four
times more fertiliser than it did ten years ago. The record 1978
harvest, if properly distributed, was sufficient to meet the food needs
of the population. Yet millions of Indians are still starving and mal-
nourished. The FAO's 4th World Food Survey estimated that, in
1971-2, 15% of the family units had less than 2000 calories per
person per day. And just as India illustrates how social inequalities
are untouched by 'development', Brazil shows how regional
inequalities within countries, as between countries, also remain
unchanged. A much quoted example of rapid industrialisation and
economic growth in the Third World, Brazil has a total calorie supply
more than sufficient for its population. Yet while in the South of Brazil
all the rural population now gets more than 2000 calories per head per
day, in the Northeast about half the people still have less than 2000
calories a day (Chonchol 1979). Both examples show that increased
production alone, even self-sufficiency on a national level, does not
stop hunger in a market economy.

By contrast, the Chinese have demonstrated how the threat of
famine can be tackled for all a nation's people. Any policy aimed at
feeding all the people of a country adequately has to start *with* those
people. It has to start by refusing to cooperate any longer with those
who drain off the wealth of the country. It has to start by giving the
land back to the people so they can grow food which *they* will eat.
Such a policy has to bring all the people into the production process,
combining their labour with full utilisation of the other available
resources to produce the food and other basic needs of the people.
Without eradication of inequalities, there can be no eradication of
hunger.

And until the food base has been secured, until what has been termed the 'famine threshold' has been passed, it is impossible to mobilise a healthy population for further development and industrialisation. This was the lesson of Europe: until the food supply had been assured by the agricultural revolution, industrialisation was impossible; in the Third World the legacy of colonialism means that such a revolution has to be even more far-reaching than was Europe's.

And, as Sir John Boyd Orr stressed in Britain in the war years, not only must the food be produced, and by that he meant the right food, the food needed by the people and not luxury or export cash-crops, but it must *get* to the people. The improved health and nutritional levels of the British people, during a period of severe shortages, were a vindication of his ideas. Whether this is achieved by rationing, or by control of harvests by producer-consumer groups rather than speculating middlemen, is a decision for the people of each country.

Forty years ago the Nazis killed 6 million people. At the Nuremberg trials those responsible claimed they personally could not be blamed, that it was the 'system', that the decisions were made higher up. This was not accepted: they were condemned. Today it is a question of perhaps 20 million dying *every year*. These deaths from starvation are also the result of a system, of deliberate policies. What can we say of those, in government, business or international agencies, who operate this system, which results in these deaths? Indeed, what can the ordinary person do?

I asked the men, 'What are you carrying wrapped in that hammock, brothers?' And they answered, 'We carry a dead body, brother.' So I asked . . . 'Was he killed or did he die a natural death?' 'That is difficult to answer, brother. It seems more to have been a murder.' 'How was the man killed? With a knife or a bullet, brothers?' I asked. 'It was neither a knife nor a bullet; it was a much more perfect crime. One that leaves no sign.' 'Then how did they kill this man?' I asked, and they calmly answered: 'This man was killed by hunger, brother.'

de Castro 1970: 102-3

It is fashionable now to question the usefulness of aid which, certainly does do more harm than good. But the real problem is elsewhere. We must understand and accept that hunger in the Third

World can be cured only by drastic social change, perhaps along lines we do not like. Our role is to stop preventing the people of the Third World from bringing about this change, to stop supporting the repressive regimes holding down the people, to stop draining off the resources the people need to develop, to stop selling irrelevant development models intended to help us rather than to help them. The people of the Third World are perfectly capable of solving their own problems, if we let them. Our job is to 'get off their backs'.

It is also our job, in the so-called 'developed' societies of the Centre, to look at our own system and ask why such intolerable inequalities remain. And to make some decisions more fundamental than which bit of the system we tinker around with next. For we have to decide whether we want to continue a pattern of domination by the few — of nature and of other human beings — or start to live *with* nature and for the benefit of *all* human beings. As Roszak says: "There are no technical answers to ethical questions."

> So much cries out to be done
> And always urgently
> The world rolls on,
> Time presses.
> Ten thousand years are too long,
> Now is the time!
>
> Mao Zedong

Annotated List of References

The following list (together with the material referred to only in the text) contains the items I found most useful in writing this book, some for the arguments put forward, some only for facts and figures. Once you've made a start it's easy to follow through the references which sound interesting in a book or article you've found valuable.

Much of this material may not be available at W.H. Smith's. If you don't have a good local bookshop try Third World Publications (151 Stratford Rd, Birmingham; SAE for catalogue). They carry a large stock and operate a (sometimes leisurely) mail order service.

If, like most of us, you can spend only a limited amount on periodicals and books, remember your local library will have access to many more books than appear on its shelves. I have no access to specialised research facilities and got much of this material on inter-library loan. I would like to record my thanks to the staff of Macclesfield Public Library who were always helpful in getting sometimes obscure books and papers very quickly.

In the following list: * = good introduction to the topic; pb = paperback.

Abdalla, Ismail-Sabri 1979: "What Development? A Third World Viewpoint" in *IFDA Dossier* 13, November
A corrective to the Western-centred viewpoints peddled by the media, giving a valuable insight into what the Third World sees as priorities.

Abelson, P.H. ed. 1975: *Food: Politics, Economics, Nutrition & Research* (American Association for the Advancement of Science, Washington DC, pb)
Articles reprinted from the AAAS journal *Science*

Allaby, M. & Allen, F. 1974: *Robots Behind the Plow: Modern Farming and the need for an Organic Alternative* (Rodale, Emmaus)
What's happening to American agriculture and what may happen to agriculture in Western Europe and a programme which would give us better food and a better society.

Arruda, Marcos ed. 1980: *Ecumenism and a New World Order: The Failure of the 1970s and the Challenge of the 1980s* (World Council of Churches, Geneva, pb)
A critical review of economic questions from the standpoint of the ecumenical movement: "development must be understood . . . as the struggle of the poor against the structures of domination and oppression."

See also the second volume: *Transnational Corporations, Technology and Human Development* (WCC, 1980, pb)

Aziz, Sartaj 1978: *Rural Development: Learning from China* (Macmillan, London, pb)

Berger, John 1979: *Pig Earth* (Writers & Readers Publishing Cooperative, London)
French peasant life. The 'Historical Afterword' is an excellent essay on the significance of the European peasantry and of their threatened elimination.

Bernton, Hal 1981: "Brazil's Alternative Moonshot" in *Harrowsmith* (Camden East, Ontario) No. 36, June-July
Describes the development of fuel distilled from sugar cane aimed at making Brazil self-sufficient in energy.

Berry, Wendell 1977: *The Unsettling of America: Culture and Agriculture* (Sierra Club, San Francisco)
A demonstration of what the US lost when it abandoned its "commitment to living well, in place, on the land" and an impassioned refutation of the concept that the supreme value is maximum production. A moving and important book.

Berthelot, J. & de Ravignan, F. 1980: *Les Sillons de la Faim* (Harmattan, Paris, pb)
Careful analysis of those political elements of the food situation sedulously avoided by the 1979 FAO conference.

Bhagavan, M.R. *et al* 1973: *The Death of the Green Revolution* (Haslemere Declaration Group & Third World First, London & Oxford, pb)
A good short exposé of the Green Revolution myth.

Borgstrom, Georg 1973: *World Food Resources* (Intertext, Aylesbury, pb).

—1973a: "Food, Feed, and Energy" in *Ambio* (Journal of the Swedish Academy of Science, Stockholm) Vol. 2 No. 6

— 1973b: "Ecological Aspects of Protein Feeding — The Case of Peru" in M.T. Farvar & J.P. Milton eds. *The Careless Technology* (Tom Stacey, London)

—1974: "The Food-Population Dilemma" in *Ambio* Vol. 3 No. 3-4
All Borgstrom's work sets the food problem into a wider perspective and emphasises the importance of food as "the key element in the present ecological crisis." Very good on the land and food (including fish) diverted from feeding Third World people to feeding the Centre's animals.

Boyce, J.K. & Hartmann, B. 1981: "Hunger in a Fertile Land" in *Ceres* Vol. 14 No. 2, March-April
Political factors behind hunger in Bangladesh.

Buchanan, Keith. 1970: *The Transformation of the Chinese Earth* (Bell, London)
Describes the processes of social and physical change by which the Chinese began to eliminate hunger.

*de Castro, Josué 1952: *The Geography of Hunger* (Gollancz, London).
Though published thirty years ago this remains the outstanding analysis of the elements in the "industry of hunger". De Castro is a former director of FAO.

—1966: *Death in the Northeast* (Random House, NY)

Injustice and destitution in Northeast Brazil.

—1970: *Of Men and Crabs* (Vanguard, NY)
Semi-autobiographical novel of hunger in the Northeast Brazilian coast-land.

*Cavadino, P. 1972: *Get off their backs!* (Vanguard, NY)

*Cavadino, P. 1972: *Get off their backs!* (Third World First, Oxford, pb)
Good short account of how the Centre uses aid, trade and investment to maintain its domination of the Third World.

CBNS 1975: Center for the Biology of Natural Systems: *A Comparison of the Production, Economic Returns, and Energy Intensiveness of Corn Belt Farms That Do and Do Not Use Inorganic Fertilisers and Pesticides* (Washington University, Saint Louis, Missouri)

CBNS 1976: *Organic and Conventional Crop Production in the Corn Belt: A Comparison of Economic Performance and Energy Use for Selected Farms* (Washington University, Saint Louis, Missouri)

Ceres: Food and Agricultural Organisation (FAO) Review on Agriculture and Development (Rome), available from HMSO.
Essential background reading on what's being done and what needs to be done. The May-June 1981 issue contained special background papers for the first World Food Day.

Chonchol, Jacques 1979: "L'alimentation mondiale: L'échec des solutions productivistes" in *IFDA Dossier* 13, November
The failure of orthodox programmes involving more finance and technology to rid the world of hunger and a criticism of wasteful over-consumption by the rich nations.

— 1979a: "Espaces ruraux et planification du développement" in *Le Monde diplomatique* July
The components of an alternative development strategy concentrating on rural areas outlined by a former minister of the Allende government in Chile.

Chopra, Pran 1981: "The paradox of Kerala" in *Ceres* Vol. 14 No. 2 March-April
Account of the beginnings of real development — reduction of social inequalities — in one of India's poorest states. Demonstrates the importance of political will and institutional factors.

CIA 1974: Central Intelligence Agency: *Potential Implications of Trends in World Population, Food Production and Climate* (Washington DC)
Cold blooded analysis of how, in an increasingly hungry world, food may become the ultimate weapon.

CIS 1975: Counter-Information Service: Anti-Report No 11: *Unilever's World* (9 Poland St, London, pb)
CIS produces excellent reports which get beyond the media's bland generalisations to the realities of power in society as manifested in big business, oil interests, unemployment etc.

Clairmonte, F. 1960: *Economic Liberalism and Underdevelopment* (Asia Publishing House, Bombay)
A scathing attack on economic liberalism and a full account of the role it played in making of India a dominated and backward society.

Cole, G.D.H. & Postgate, R. 1938: *The Common People 1746-1938* (Methuen, London)
One of the first books dealing with history from the point of view of those who underwent it rather than those who made it.

Commoner, B. 1972: *The Closing Circle* (Cape, London)
How humanity's neglect of basic ecological principles has diminished the habitat of all living things.

Cottrell, F. 1955: *Energy and Society* (McGraw Hill, NY)
Contains useful data on energy inputs into agricultural systems.

Dennis, H. 1979: "The Third World: Our Dump for Dangerous Products?" in *Not Man Apart* (Friends of the Earth, San Francisco) December
A brief account of some of the issues dealt with by Weir and Schapiro.

Dumont, Rene 1957: *Types of Rural Economy* (English translation, Methuen, London)
— 1965: *Lands Alive* (English translation, Monthly Review, London)
*— & Cohen, N. 1980: *The Growth of Hunger* (Marion Boyars, London, pb)
— & Mottin, M.F. 1980: *L'Afrique etranglee* (Seuil, Paris, pb). Dumont is the world's greatest agronomist. His studies of Third World peasants — "the true proletarians of our time" — spell out the human costs of underdevelopment — and our responsibilities.

Evans, George Ewart 1956: *Ask the Fellows who Cut the Hay* (Faber, London, pb)
The rural societies of Britain before the tractor replaced the horse as recorded in the oral traditions of East Anglian farm workers.

FAO 1977: *The 4th World Food Survey* (Rome, pb)
The official UN overview of the world agriculture and nutrition situation providing basic statistics and commentary.

FEA: *The Far East & Australia* 1976-77 edition; a yearbook published by Europa Publications, London

Feder, Ernest 1980: "The Odious Competition Between Man and Animal over Agricultural Resources in the Underdeveloped Countries" in *Review* (Binghampton, NY) Vol. II No. 3
Ethical implications of the developed societies' use of Third World land for export-oriented meat production.

Freire, Paulo 1974: "Extension or Communication" in *Education for Critical Consciousness* (Sheed & Ward, London)
Sees extension work as a form of domination rather than as liberating peasants so that they can transform their own lives.

The Future in our Hands: Movement for a new life-style and a fair distribution of the world's resources. (Framtiden i Vare Hender, Torggata 35, Oslo – 1, Norway)
Grew out of a book of the same title by Erik Dammann (Gyldendal 1972; published in Britain by Pergamon)

Galeano, Eduardo 1973: *The Open Veins of Latin America: Five Centuries of the Pillage of a Continent* (Monthly Review, NY & London)
Biting account of how colonialism and neocolonialism have warped the societies of Latin America.

*George, Susan 1976: *How the Other Half Dies: The Real Reasons for World Hunger* (Penguin, Harmondsworth, pb)
Essential reading. Lively and careful documentation of the processes and institutions which have turned an era of potential plenty into an era of endemic hunger.

*— 1979: *Feeding the Few: Corporate Control of Food* (Institute for Policy Studies, Washington DC & Amsterdam, pb)
Excellent discussion of the "takeover of Third World food systems, designed in the image of the developed countries and for their benefit" and the implications for basic food supplies.

Goldstein, J. ed. 1973: *The New Food Chain: An Organic Link Between Farm and City* (Rodale, Emmaus)
Essays on the city-farm relationship, the link between organic farming and economic stability and "the safety of our foods and the life expectancy of our environments". American, but relevant to all developed societies.

Green, R.H. & Seidman, A. 1968: *Unity or Poverty? The Economics of Pan-Africanism* (Penguin, Harmondsworth, pb)

*Harrison, Paul 1980: *The Third World Tomorrow* (Penguin, Harmondsworth, pb)
Readable look at Third World development with lots of facts and case studies by an experienced journalist.

Harrison, Ruth 1964: *Animal Machines: The New Factory Farming System* (Vincent Stuart, London)
The cost, in terms of cruelty to animals (and diminished nutritional value for people), of intensive meat and egg production.

Hightower, Jim 1975: *Eat Your Heart Out: Food Profiteering in America* (Crown, NY)
The movement of big business into food production and marketing and the disastrous impact for both farmers and consumers.

Hunter, Neale 1970: "The Good Earth & the Good Society" in B. Douglass & R. Terrill eds. *China & Ourselves* (Beacon Press, Boston)

ICIDI 1980: Independent Commission on International Development Issues (Chairman: Willy Brandt): *North-South: A Programme for Survival* (Pan, London, pb). Also known as "The Brandt Report".
Report on, and proposals to overcome, inequality around the world. A less than radical analysis but a useful source of facts and statistics. For an alternative view see Teresa Hayter's reply to the Brandt Report: *The Creation of World Poverty* (Pluto, London, pb)

IFDA: International Foundation for Development Alternatives: *IFDA Dossier* (2 place du marché, Nyon, Switzerland)
The *Dossiers* provide a regular flow of excellent and wide-ranging essays on all aspects of development; especially valuable for contributions from Third World citizens.

IFDP: Institute for Food & Development Policy (1885 Mission St, San Francisco). Established by Frances Moore Lappé and Joseph Collins to continue — and widen — the work started with *Food First*.

Illich, Ivan 1971: *Celebration of Awareness* (Calder & Boyars, London, pb)

*ILO 1979: International Labour Office: *Profiles of Rural Poverty*: "A

popularised version of *Poverty & Landlessness in Rural Asia* with additional material on Africa & Latin America". (ILO, Geneva, pb)
Good short account which shows that unequal distribution of land and other productive assets is the main cause of poverty.

Knight, E. & Rotha, P. 1945: *World of Plenty* (Nicholson & Watson, London, pb)
The book of the wartime film about Food — Man's Security Number One. The idealism did not survive the Cold War.

*Lappé, F.M. & Collins, J. 1977: *Food First: Beyond the Myth of Scarcity* (Houghton Mifflin, Boston) Now also available as a pb.
Excellent, question-and-answer format, introduction to the world food problem.

— 1977: "The Eight Myths of Hunger" in *Ceres* July-August
A useful 7 page summary of some of the ideas in *Food First.*

*— & Kinley, D. 1980: *Aid as Obstacle* (IFDP, San Francisco, pb)
Excellent analysis of why aid doesn't help the hungry. Discusses the institutions and power structures which manipulate aid for political ends.

Leach, G. 1975: *Energy and Food Production* (International Institute for Environment & Development, London Washington DC, pb)
Energy input and output of UK agriculture with detailed analyses of energy costs not only of producing food but getting it from farm to table.

Malik, Baljit 1980: "An Asian Panorama of Peasant Oppression" in *IFDA Dossier* 19, Sept/Oct
The gross inequalities in the agrarian systems of Asia and the suppression by state agencies of peasant organisations working for change.

Manas: "A journal of Independent Inquiry" (P.O. Box 32112, El Sereno Station, Los Angeles) Weekly
Wide-ranging and stimulating essays and reviews covering human societies in their relationships with one another and their natural environment.

Meillassoux, C. 1974: "Development or Exploitation: Is the Sahel Famine Good for Business" in *Review of African Political Economy* (London) No. 1

*Merrill, R. ed. 1976: *Radical Agriculture* (Harper & Row, NY, pb)
Well documented studies of agribusiness in the US, of the radical alternative to agribusiness and of a self-sustaining agriculture which would provide the basis for a healthy rural community.

*Mooney, P.R. (1979): *Seeds of the Earth: A Private or Public Resource* (Inter Pares, Ottawa, for the Canadian Council for International Co-operation and the International Coalition for Development Action, Bedford Chambers, Covent Garden, London, pb)
The importance of the genetic base of the world's food supply and the implications of the growing control of agribusiness over this vital part of the food system.

Muller, Mike 1974: *The Baby Killer* (War on Want, London, pb)
The report which exposed how TNCs like Nestles, by promoting powdered milk as a substitute for breast milk, contributed to increased infant mortality in the Third World. The longer follow-up volume by Andy Chetley (*The Baby Killer Scandal* 1979) shows that profits continue to be

more important to TNCs than the health of children.

NACLA Report: published by the North American Congress on Latin America (151 West 19th St, 9th Floor, New York, 10011)
Committed, well-documented articles on Latin American development and US role/interference.

*New Internationalist: 374 Wandsworth Road, London SW9
Illustrated, readable periodical; each month provides a good introduction to a different development issue. The Sept 1977 issue was a cartoon version of Lappé & Collins' *Food First*.

Nyerere, J.K. 1979: "On Rural Development", address to the FAO World Conference on Agrarian Reform & Rural Development, July; reprinted in *IFDA Dossier* 11, September.

Odum, H. 1973: "Energy, Ecology & Economics" in *Ambio* (Stockholm) Vol. 2 No. 6
Valuable discussion of the limits to rapid growth in any sector of the economy and convincing arguments for the need for a return to a steady state economy.

OECD 1979: Interfutures: *Facing the Future: mastering the probable & managing the unpredictable* (Paris, pb)
A long review of world prospects; useful for facts and statistics and for learning what those who manage society have in store for us.

O'Keefe, P., Westgate, K., & Wisner, B. 1976: "Taking the Naturalness out of natural disasters" in *Nature* Vol. 260, April 15
How the organisation of societies affects their vulnerability to such things as climatic variability or earthquakes.

Palmer, Ingrid, 1972: *Food and the new agricultural technology* (UNRISD, Geneva, pb)
A study of the, usually negative, impact of the Green Revolution on nutrition in the Third World. UNRISD material is among the best of the official UN-type studies, going well beyond straight documentation.

Payer, Cheryl 1979: "The World Bank and the Small Farmers" in *Journal of Peace Research* Vol. XVI No. 4
Argues that World Bank lending to 'small farmers' is designed to force self-provisioning peasants into the market economy; and that what the rural poor need is not cash but support for their own initiatives to liberate themselves.

Pirie, N.W. 1969: *Food Resources: Conventional & Novel* (Penguin, Harmondsworth, pb)
Discusses the capabilities of conventional agriculture to feed the world and argues for the use of a much wider range of plant, marine and animal products.

Power, J. 1975: "The Alternative to Starvation" in *Encounter* November

**Pyke, M. 1970: *Man and Food* (Weidenfeld & Nicolson, London, pb)
Illustrated introduction to the chemistry of food, nutrition and food technology. Relates the academic facts to the sociology of famine and malnutrition.

**Robbins, C. & Ansari, J. 1976: *The Profits of Doom* (War on Want, London, pb)

Good short look at the economic and political reasons for hunger.

Sharma, Hari P. 1973: "The Green Revolution in India: Prelude to a Red One?" in K. Gough & H.P. Sharma eds. *Imperialism and Revolution in South Asia* (Monthly Review, NY & London)
Good discussion of the failure of land reform, the growing inequality in rural India which has accompanied the GR, and the resulting politicisation of the peasantry.

Shoard, Marion 1980: *The Theft of the Countryside* (Temple Smith, London, pb)
Disturbing, well documented account of the ecological damage wrought by profit-oriented farming in Britain (backed by lavish government subsidies).

Sider, R.J. 1977: *Rich Christians in an Age of Hunger: A Biblical Study* Hodder & Stoughton, London, pb)
An excellent challenge to Christians: the facts about poverty and affluence; the Bible's attitude to the poor and possessions; the Christian response.

South: The Third World Magazine (London, monthly)
Early issues useful.

Spitz, Pierre 1981: "Livelihood & the Food Squeeze" in *Ceres* May-June
The need for social change and greater reliance on peasant knowledge if hunger is to be conquered.

Stavis, B. 1975: "How China is Solving its Food Problem" in *Bulletin of Concerned Asian Scholars* (San Francisco) July-Sept
Useful account of how one nation began to solve its food problem.

Steinhart, J.S. & Steinhart, C.D. 1975: "Energy Use in the US Food System" in Abelson *op. cit.*

Strahm, R.H. 1975: *Pourquoi sont-ils si pauvres?* (Baconnière, Neuchâtel, Suisse, pb)
57 excellent diagrams with brief commentary, showing the relationship between over- and under-development.

*Taylor, J.V. 1975: *Enough is Enough* (SCM, London, pb)
Highly readable denunciation of the way in which the manipulated wants of the wealthy take bread out of the mouths of the poor; and suggestions of what we can do in our own lives.

Trowell, H. 1974: "Obesity in the western world" in *Plant foods for man*, Vol. 1 Pt 3/4

*Tudge, Colin 1979: *The Famine Business* (Penguin, Harmondsworth, pb)
A lucid account of the interrelations between obesity and hunger and a forceful argument for rethinking our agricultural and dietary patterns.

War on Want: 467 Caledonian Rd, London

Weir, D. & Schapiro, M. 1981: *Circle of Poison: Pesticides and People in a Hungry World* (IFDP, San Francisco, pb)
Documents the international marketing of restricted pesticides, their lethal impact (especially on Third World peasants), and how these poisons come back into the developed nations in the foods they import from the Third World. Excellent.

Wheelwright, E.L. 1968: "Historical Appraisal: Colonialism — Past and Present" in Japan Economic Research Centre: *Structure & Development in Asian Economies* (JERC, Tokyo, pb)

Well documented account of how colonialism creates underdevelopment; especially useful on India.

*Whittemore, Claire 1981: *Land for People: Land Tenure and the Very Poor* (Oxfam Public Affairs Unit, Oxford, pb)
Important and well documented demonstration of thesis that the chief causes of hunger are "unjust land tenure systems and the political, economic and social policies which enable these systems to prevail."

Wilkinson, R.G. 1976: "Dear David Ennals . . ." in *New Society* 16 Dec
Demonstrates how in Britain (as in the Third World) health and expectation of life depend on quality of diet and this in turn on income and social status.

Woodham-Smith, C. 1964: *The Great Hunger* (Readers Union/Hamish Hamilton, London)
The classic account of the Irish famine and its underlying social causes.

World Bank 1980: *World Development Report 1980* (OUP, Oxford & NY, pb)
Most useful for the tables which give all the basic global statistics relating to development.

World Council of Churches: 150 route de Ferney, 1211 Geneva 20
Publishes some excellent material on development. See, eg, their Programme on Transnational Corporations' Bulletin *Sharing*; the August 1981 issue, "The Transnationalization of Latin America . . ." is a good example of radical Christian involvement in social issues.

The novel or short story can often convey the reality and processes of oppression more vividly than the academic text. In addition to those quoted the following are recommended:

Alegria, Ciro 1941: *Broad and Alien is the World* (NY); South America

Chand, Prem 1962: *A Handful of Wheat and Other Stories* (trans by P.C. Gupta, New Delhi); India

Charhadi, Driss ben Hamed 1964: *A Life Full of Holes* (Intro by Paul Bowles, London); North Africa

Hanley, James 1951: *Consul at Sunset* (London); Africa

King, Evan 1956: *Children of the Black Haired People* (London); China

And to remind us that the processes of rural oppression are not confined to the Third World:

Agee, James & Evans, Walker 1969: *Let us now praise famous men* (Panther, London, pb)

Smith, Iain Crichton 1968: *Consider the Lilies* (Gollancz, London)